Why We're Losing the War on Terror

TONBRIDGE SCHOOL LIBRARY

R58695J0502

Why We're Losing the War on Terror

PAUL ROGERS

polity

Copyright © Paul Rogers 2008

The right of Paul Rogers to be identified as Author of this Work has been asserted in accordance with the UK Copyright, Designs and Patents Act 1988.

First published in 2008 by Polity Press

Reprinted 2008

Polity Press
65 Bridge Street
Cambridge CB2 1UR, UK.

Polity Press
350 Main Street
Malden, MA 02148, USA

All rights reserved. Except for the quotation of short passages for the purpose of criticism and review, no part of this publication may be reproduced, stored in a retrieval system, or transmitted, in any form or by any means, electronic, mechanical, photocopying, recording or otherwise, without the prior permission of the publisher.

ISBN-13: 978-07456-4196-6
ISBN-13: 978-07456-4197-3 (pb)

A catalogue record for this book is available from the British Library.

Typeset in 10.25 on 13 pt FF Scala
by Servis Filmsetting Ltd, Manchester
Printed and bound in Great Britain by MPG Books Ltd, Bodmin, Cornwall

The publisher has used its best endeavours to ensure that the URLs for external websites referred to in this book are correct and active at the time of going to press. However, the publisher has no responsibility for the websites and can make no guarantee that a site will remain live or that the content is or will remain appropriate.

Every effort has been made to trace all copyright holders, but if any have been inadvertently overlooked the publishers will be pleased to include any necessary credits in any subsequent reprint or edition.

For further information on Polity, visit our website: www.polity.co.uk

320.973
R S 86195 J

Contents

Acknowledgements

Although I take full responsibility for this book, it does arise, in part, from many discussions in recent years. These include frequent lectures at defence colleges and work with a wide range of political and non-governmental organizations, especially a close involvement with Open Democracy and Oxford Research Group. It has been particularly helpful to be working at Bradford University's Department of Peace Studies – the extraordinary range of staff and students, drawn from more than forty countries, has provided an immensely experienced and thoroughly stimulating environment. Finally, I would like to thank Louise Knight of Polity for originally suggesting that I have a go at writing this book, and Louise and her colleagues, especially Emma Hutchinson and Gail Ferguson, for their help in seeing it through to completion.

Paul Rogers,
Bradford,
July 2007

Preface: Lost Cause or Second Chance?

As the Iraq War entered its fifth year in March 2007, the United States was engaged in a new effort to contain the insurgency. Following numerous predictions from the Bush administration since the start of the war that military forces would soon be scaled down, the reverse was happening, with a 'surge' of 30,000 troops taking the total deployment in Iraq to over 160,000. As this got under way, the US Department of Defense also announced an increase in US troop numbers in Afghanistan, where close to 30,000 troops were deployed with forces from other NATO states in an effort to counter a Taliban revival across much of southern Afghanistan.

The wars in both countries showed no sign of easing and constituted a predicament for the United States that was in marked contrast to the expectations five years earlier. Then, a 'war on terror' had been declared in response to the 9/11 atrocities. The aims of that war had evolved over a few months from an initial operation to terminate the Taliban regime in Afghanistan and cripple the al-Qaida movement to a much larger endeavour that took in an 'axis of evil' of three rogue states, Iraq, Iran and North Korea. All of these were seen as having entirely unacceptable regimes that both supported terrorism and were bent on developing weapons of mass destruction.

In early 2002, expectations in Washington were high that post-Taliban Afghanistan would be a stable pro-western state that would enable the United States to increase its influence in the region, both by a direct involvement in the country and also through improved links with several Central Asian states. Having lost its main area of operations, the al-Qaida movement had been dispersed and there was every hope that Osama bin Laden and other leaders would soon be detained or killed. Furthermore, there was a confident expectation within the Bush administration that the Saddam Hussein regime in Iraq could be terminated, if need be by military force. A new pro-western government espousing liberal-market economics would have an excellent relationship with Washington, and American influence in the oil-rich region of the Persian Gulf would be substantially enhanced.

Even more valuable would be the indirect pressure that this would put on the regime in Tehran. With Afghanistan to the east and Iraq to the west both experiencing regime change, and with pro-western governments in power, Iran's position in the region would be much diminished, quite possibly rendering regime change in Tehran unnecessary. More generally, the robust and single-minded response to the 9/11 attacks could well set in motion regime change across the Middle East, ushering in a period of enhanced pro-western governance. This, in turn, would be an important step in achieving the ideal of a New American Century, a concept beloved of the neoconservatives and assertive realists who were so prominent in the Bush administration.

Instead of realizing these dreams, the first six years of the war on terror have shown the idea of the New American Century boosted by the war on terror to be something of a lost cause. In the two wars, over 3,500 US troops have been killed and more than 25,000 seriously wounded, many of the latter maimed for life. The war in Afghanistan shows no sign of ending, with record opium poppy crops supporting an illicit economy that helps fuel the insurgency. In Iraq there have been at least 100,000 civilians killed and close to four million Iraqis are refugees. A bitter anti-American mood is evident across the Middle East and beyond, and the much-vaunted coalition of like-minded states in Iraq is reduced to a rump – a few thousand troops, many of them British, remain there but most countries have quietly withdrawn. Even in the United States, efforts to link Iraq with the wider war on terror have proved increasingly difficult, and the Republican Party lost control of Congress in November 2006 following political campaigning in which Iraq loomed large. Most surprising of all, the al-Qaida movement has proved unexpectedly resilient, having dispersed from its original bases in Afghanistan to function as a near-virtual entity, even if it does have distinct centres in western Pakistan.

This book is concerned with a preliminary analysis of the early years of the war on terror and why the policies adopted by the United States and its closest coalition partners have failed to achieve their aims. It attempts to do so in three phases. Part I examines the context of the period, starting with an assessment of the relevant features of US politics in the years leading up to 9/11. This covers the particular outlook of the Bush administration in relation to foreign and defence policy, and seeks to examine the extent to which the neoconservative tendency was particularly relevant in determining the response to 9/11. It also explores the military context by reviewing the major changes in the US military posture during the 1990s. By the start of the new century, the United States was clearly the world's sole superpower and was deploying military forces of unparalleled capability. It was the only country remotely capable of fighting the global war on terror in the manner envisaged, and its capabilities did much to ensure precisely how and where that war might be fought.

Finally, Part I engages with the highly relevant issue of US oil security and the significance of the Persian Gulf reserves – easily the largest in the world. The argument is not that the United States went into Iraq to 'grab' that country's oil, even though Iraq did have reserves that were at least four times larger than the entire US domestic reserves, including Alaska. At the same time, it most certainly is argued that the sixty-year history of US military concern with the security of the Persian Gulf is highly relevant in understanding recent operations.

Part II reviews the developments in Afghanistan and Iraq, and also the attempts to counter the al-Qaida movement, setting the aims of the operations against the outcomes so far and offering an analysis of some of the main reasons why the outcome of the war on terror is proving to be so different to the early expectations.

Finally, Part III looks at the consequences of US policy and then seeks to assess whether other policies might have been, and might still be, more appropriate. It does so with specific reference to Iraq, Afghanistan and the al-Qaida movement, but goes beyond this to question whether the failures of recent years might actually prompt a more fundamental reassessment of a western security posture that might best be described as a 'control paradigm'. In particular, is this posture in any way appropriate to a global system in which the major security issues of the next few decades are likely to arise from a dangerously widening socio-economic divide interacting with environmental constraints, especially climate change? Would it be more appropriate to move towards a 'sustainable security' paradigm and, if so, might the failure of the war on terror make it more likely that such a change will come about?

Sustainable security is concerned with developing a security outlook that recognizes the centrality of a human security concept rooted in justice and emancipation, accepts that global issues such as socio-economic divisions and environmental constraints require a common security approach more than a state-centric model, and also accepts the requirement to ensure that policies adopted are sustainable in that they do not create new forms of insecurity in responding to short-term predicaments. This book concludes by arguing that this is the appropriate model for the future and that the very failure of the control paradigm that has been at the centre of the war on terror does at least mean that space has opened up for the vigorous pursuit of alternatives. That will do nothing to redress the violence, suffering and misery occasioned by the conduct of the war, but it might at least help prevent even greater problems in the future.

PART I
Context

CHAPTER ONE

The Political Context

History repeated

Before the election of President George W. Bush in November 2000, oppositional politics in the United States in the late 1990s bore some striking similarities to the politics of the late 1970s. In each period, powerful Republican groups were advocating major changes in direction in US foreign and security policy against incumbent Democrat administrations; on each occasion these groups achieved their aims and each time they were able to move into positions of considerable authority and influence.

In the late 1970s, President Jimmy Carter was facing vocal and determined opposition to his relatively liberal foreign policy, especially concerning his relations with the Soviet Union. Although the Soviet leadership was increasingly moribund, the detente of the early 1960s had long been replaced by growing tensions made worse by the development of new military technologies, not least highly accurate multi-warhead nuclear missiles. While the United States could not claim to be behind the Soviets in terms of technology, major claims were made by right-wing groups that the Soviet Union was narrowing the US technological lead while producing new nuclear and conventional weapons at a far higher rate.

A number of think tanks and interest groups were particularly active from around 1977 onwards, especially the Committee on the Present Danger, the John Birch Society, High

Frontier and the American Enterprise Institute. Their campaigning focused largely on the requirement to 'rearm America' in the face of an increasing threat from the Soviet Union, a campaigning process that gained substantial strength in the run-up to the November 1980 presidential election through two entirely unexpected events. The first was the Soviet occupation of Afghanistan in support of a communist regime in Kabul. This was seen as an unambiguous example of Soviet expansionism, and one that threatened Pakistan and might eventually give the Soviet Union direct access through Baluchistan to a warm-water port in the Indian Ocean.

The second development was only indirectly concerned with the Cold War confrontation but had an even greater effect on US politics. The fall of the Shah of Iran and the subsequent Iranian Revolution brought to power a radical Islamic theocracy that was deeply opposed to the United States and its interests in the region. The Iranian Revolution was a shock on three quite different counts. One was the sheer rapidity of the change. US intelligence agencies and diplomats got virtually no warning of the massive changes, having almost entirely failed to recognize the nature of the tensions developing in Iranian society and the deepening opposition to the autocratic rule of the Shah.

The Iranian Revolution was also a deep shock because of the role that the Shah's Iran had played in US regional security policy. Under the Shah, Iran had been seen as a key bulwark against any Soviet military action that might be directed against Persian Gulf oil reserves in the event of an east–west confrontation. While the Soviet Union was easily self-sufficient in oil supplies, the possibility that it could gain direct control of Persian Gulf oil reserves was a serious concern among US military planners. Fortunately, the presence of Iran, with its modern western armaments and large armed forces, did much to reduce concern. The sudden loss of this key regional ally was thus a severe shock.

Finally, the holding of over fifty US diplomats hostage for 444 days in 1979–81 during the Revolution was an even greater shock; indeed it was an affront to US political sensibilities, made worse by the failure of a military operation, Eagle Claw, to release them.[1] Afghanistan and Iran may have made it difficult for President Carter to gain re-election in 1980, but the right-wing interest groups added to his difficulties, especially as they seemed to strike a chord with American public opinion, increasing support for Ronald Reagan.

President Reagan took office in 1981 and appointed to his administration many of the key people in the interest groups that had highlighted the rearming agenda. With rhetoric that included the concept of the Soviet bloc as an 'evil empire', the United States increased its military spending and the Cold War entered one of its most dangerous phases. For four years in the early 1980s, a Soviet Union with a largely moribund leadership struggled to match the United States in military developments, a situation that only changed after Mikhail Gorbachev came to power in 1985. With the collapse of the Soviet Union at the end of the decade, many of those who had advocated the rearming agenda considered themselves vindicated and some began to see the possibility not so much of George H. W. Bush's 'New World Order' of the early 1990s, but of a much more global role for the United States in the new century that was approaching.

A New American Century

Although aspects of the 1991 Gulf War were a shock to US military planners, especially the problem of the Scud missiles and the Iraqi chemical and biological weapons programme (explored in chapter 2), in most other respects the decade of the 1990s was one of consolidation of the international system into a unipolar order. The United States experienced a military setback in Somalia in 1993, engaged in action with NATO states in the Balkans, and experienced the early effects of radical Islamic paramilitary action in Saudi Arabia, Kenya and Tanzania, but in virtually all other respects the decade demonstrated the power of the United States and the perceived success of the American political and economic system. The Soviet bloc had imploded at the start of the decade and China was progressively embracing elements of the free market. Both developments seemed to demonstrate the complete failure of communism, implying that western-style free market liberalism was the only workable model.

However much this might be criticized by activists in western states, and however much an increasingly vocal anti-globalization movement might point to the failures of a globalized market to promote emancipation, there was a far stronger community of opinion formers in the United States who saw the twenty-first century as a remarkable opportunity for the United States to mould the entire world economy in its own image. Working with close economic allies, the driving force for this new century was a deep-seated conviction that there was only one economic system, itself set in one particular political context. The system was the globalized free market and the context was liberal democracy. The collapse of the Soviet bloc showed powerfully that the only other option was a dismal failure. Moreover, there was a clear-cut choice with no realistic third way. Mixed economies that maintained substantial elements of nationalized industries and costly social welfare systems were at best inefficient and at worst politically dubious.

The political stance of what was commonly called neoconservatism or American unilateralism went much further than this in terms of a belief that the United States had an historic mission to be a civilizing force in world affairs. History was at an end in that, with the ending of the Cold War, the American way of life was now predominant. This did not imply a direct neo-colonial control of the world, but more a shaping, through governmental, business and other processes, of a world economy and polity that was broadly in the US image.

If the conservative interest groups of the late 1970s were engaged in empowering the United States to rearm and face down the Soviet Union, the equivalent groups of the late 1990s were concerned with the very reshaping of the world economic and political system, a grand project for a new American century. Perhaps the best example of this world-view was, indeed, the 'Project for the New American Century' (PNAC), established in Washington in 1997.[2] It sought from the start to distinguish itself from traditional Republican policy, pointing out that while American foreign and defence policy was adrift, and conservatives were criticizing the Clinton administration for its incoherence, such conservatives seemed unable to provide a vigorous alternative. They might resist a fall back into isolationism but had no strategic vision of America's place in the world, had internal divisions over tactics and failed to back a defence budget that 'would maintain American security and advance American interests in the new century'.[3]

In its *Statement of Principles* (3 June 1997), the Project made its aims clear:

> We aim to change this. We aim to make the case and rally support for American global leadership.
>
> As the 20th century draws to a close, the United States stands as the world's pre-eminent power. Having led the West to victory in the Cold War, America faces an opportunity and a challenge: Does the United States have the vision to build upon the achievements of past decades? Does the United States have the resolve to shape a new century favorable to American principles and interests?[4]

In opposing the Clinton administration and criticizing traditional American conservatives, the Project's supporters talked of the dangers of living off the capital of past administrations, especially in relation to military investments and foreign policy successes. There was little mention of the first Bush administration from 1989 to 1993, but a continual harking back to the golden years of Ronald Reagan: 'We seem to have forgotten the essential elements of the Reagan Administration's success: a military that is strong and ready to meet both present and future challenges; a foreign policy that boldly and purposefully promotes American principles abroad; and national leadership that accepts the United States' global responsibilities.'[5]

For the Project, there were powerful lessons to be learnt from twentieth-century failures to pre-empt threats, and a profound need to 'embrace the cause of American leadership'. The Project's *Statement of Principles* concluded by drawing out four principles:

- we need to increase defence spending significantly if we are to carry out our global responsibilities today and modernize our armed forces for the future;
- we need to strengthen our ties to democratic allies and to challenge regimes hostile to our interests and values;
- we need to promote the cause of political and economic freedom abroad;
- we need to accept responsibility for America's unique role in preserving and extending an international order friendly to our security, our prosperity, and our principles.

Such a Reaganite policy of military strength and moral clarity may not be fashionable today. But it is necessary if the United States is to build on the successes of this century and to ensure our security and greatness in the next.[6]

What is particularly striking about the vision of a New American Century as it was developed in the mid- and late 1990s was the degree of confidence and single-minded belief in the way forward. There was a marked refusal in the more forceful business and political circles to accept that there could be any legitimate alternative. It was simply unthinkable, not least because to accept the possibility of alternatives implied that the dominant model might not be fully valid. Given the abject failure of the competing paradigm of Soviet communism, there could not be any alternative. Indeed, to accept any other approach had at least to be deeply wrong-headed if not malign.

Some concerns remained as the 2000 presidential election campaign took shape, with a particular worry about the state of affairs in the Persian Gulf, especially the status of the Saddam Hussein regime. More generally, there was an unease about poorly defined threats from terrorist groups, especially those associated with attacks in Saudi Arabia and the East African embassy bombings. Russia was still having formidable difficulties in escaping from the economic disasters of the early and mid-1990s, but while that threat may have gone, other indistinct threats appeared to be evolving. As presidential contender George W. Bush put it in a campaign speech in early 2000: '... it was a dangerous world and we knew exactly who the "they" were. It was us versus them and we knew exactly who them was. Today we're not so sure who the "they" are, but we know they're there.'

The 2000 election and unilateralism

The disputed 2000 presidential election was eventually awarded to George W. Bush through a decision of the US Supreme Court, following controversy over aspects of the voting, especially the Florida 'chads'. Bush gained a smaller number of actual votes than Al Gore but succeeded in gaining victory through the Electoral College. Given the narrowness of his victory, there was a widespread assumption that he would embark on what was described at the time as a 'consensus presidency', seeking to modify some of the policies previously announced in an attempt to consolidate the authority of his administration. In practice, this was not politically necessary, given the strength of the Republican Party in the US Congress, and any sense of seeking consensus was quickly abandoned, especially in relation to foreign and security policy.

Just as Ronald Reagan had taken many of the supporters of the 'rearming America' movement into his administration, so President Bush did likewise with the neoconservatives in forming his administration in January 2001. In one respect, the Project for the New American Century already had one convinced supporter in a position of power, as Dick Cheney had run on the vice-presidential ticket in the 2000 campaign, but many other PNAC signatories also moved into the administration. Among them was the new Secretary of Defense, Donald Rumsfeld, and his deputy, Paul Wolfowitz. I. Lewis Libby took up a key role in the Vice-President's office, Elliott Abrams and Eliot A. Cohen both acquired substantial influence and Zalmay Khalilzad would eventually become Ambassador in Afghanistan and later Iraq. By no means all of these people would describe themselves as neoconservatives, a more accurate label being assertive nationalist or assertive realist, but there was a common and deep-felt belief in the potential for a New American Century and a determination to have a major impact on US foreign and security policy very early in the new administration.

One particular issue was that the United States should not be hindered in its pursuit of global leadership by unnecessary multilateral agreements, especially in the area of arms control but extending to wider issues of international security. In the first eight months of the administration, there were many examples of movement away from previous or planned agreements. President Clinton had refrained from sending the Comprehensive Nuclear Test Ban Treaty to Congress for ratification, in part because this would almost certainly have been blocked by Republicans. After the 2000 election, there was simply no chance whatsoever of ratification – it was no longer an issue. In Geneva, there was an attempt to start negotiations to prevent an arms race in space, but the United States was opposed to this, as it was to aspects of the planned International Criminal Court. The Bush administration also raised difficulties in relation to the banning of anti-personnel landmines and attempts to limit transfers of conventional armaments and made it clear that it would, in due course, withdraw from the 1972 Anti-Ballistic Missile Treaty as part of a process of building a new missile defence system for the continental United States.

For some European states, a major concern in 2001 was that the United States was beginning to show a reluctance to work towards strengthening the 1972 Biological and Toxin Weapons Convention (BTWC). This convention was important to a number of countries. The original 1972 agreement had been a convention in the correct sense of the word in that it involved a complete ban on the production, stockpiling and use of biological weapons and bio-toxins, but its core problem was that there were no verification or inspection procedures built in – it was a paper treaty, no more. More than twenty years after the 1972 BTWC, in the mid-1990s, there had been the successful completion of the Chemical Weapons Convention which was notable in having such a verification regime with an international organization to implement the procedures. This gave a model for a strengthened bio-weapons convention and negotiations started in Geneva at the end of the decade. Progress was slow and the talks lasted more than six years.[7]

In the end they were effectively killed by opposition from the Bush administration, partly on the grounds that intrusive inspection would threaten the commercial confidentiality of US biotech companies. It is fair to say that some other countries were not too disappointed that the United States should take this view, but independent analysts that were close to the negotiations were bitterly critical of the failure to improve the treaty. Their concern was that rapid developments in the areas of genetic manipulation and biotechnology could well make biological warfare a realistic military option within a few years; failing to strengthen the treaty would hinder any attempts to counter this trend.

One further example of US unilateralism was an even greater surprise to many European allies – the Bush administration's decision to withdraw from the Kyoto climate change protocols. The very idea of climate change being a significant phenomenon, let alone one related to the burning of fossil fuels, was anathema to the Bush administration, whereas it had been very largely accepted across most of Europe. Of all the unilateral moves in early 2001, this was the matter which raised most concern in Europe.

Even so, the Bush administration was very much set on this path, its attitude being admirably described by Charles Krauthammer, just a couple of months before the 9/11 attacks.

> Multipolarity, yes, when there is no alternative. But not when there is. Not when we have the unique imbalance of power that we enjoy today – and that has given the international system a stability and essential tranquillity that it had not known for at least a century.
>
> The international environment is far more likely to enjoy peace under a single hegemon. Moreover, we are not just any hegemon. We run a uniquely benign imperium.[8]

Krauthammer neatly encapsulates the attitude of the Bush administration and its neoconservative supporters in the period immediately preceding the 9/11 attacks, and it is not greatly surprising that the reaction to those attacks should have been so vigorous. Even so, in understanding the evolution of the war on terror, especially its extension to Iraq, two other factors within US politics have to be taken into account, one concerning US–Israeli relations, and the other being a strong emphasis on the need to terminate the Saddam Hussein regime in Iraq, an emphasis that was very much in evidence well before George Bush had been elected.

Christian Zionism and US–Israel relations

While sympathy for the State of Israel stretches across the US political spectrum, it is centred on the Israel lobby which has traditionally drawn much of its support from the American Jewish community. Although numbering little more than six million people, American Jews were for many years unequivocal in their support for Israel, particularly in the early post-independence years when Israel had little in the way of backing from western governments, including the United States. The US Israel lobby gained more governmental support with the rise of Arab nationalism in the 1950s and the growing perception of Israel as a bulwark against Soviet influence across the region. The Six Day War of 1967 was seen as the high point of Israeli consolidation and the potentially disastrous Yom Kippur–Ramadan War six years later was an occasion for immediate and substantial US military aid.

Given that much of the American Jewish community has liberal political views and tends to support the Democrats, it is not surprising that there were increasingly mixed feelings towards Israeli administrations in the 1980s and 1990s. Issues such as the controversial growth of settlements across the West Bank and the vigour with which the first intifada was suppressed caused much disquiet, and this intensified in reaction to policies at the end of the 1990s, especially after the start of the second intifada. While Israel was still reasonably secure in the extent of support from the US government, it was less clear that Jewish community support could be taken for granted. Fortunately for organizations such as the America

Israel Public Affairs Committee (AIPAC), another base of support had developed and came to be as significant as more traditional constituencies.

Within some sectors of evangelical Christianity, Christian Zionism has been an aspect with very clear-cut biblical roots although most students of religion would date it back to the thoughts and preachings of a Plymouth Brethren minister, John Nelson Darby (1800–1882), especially his studies at Trinity College Dublin in the early 1820s. His ideas took particular root in the United States later in the nineteenth century, especially around the time of the Biblical Conference Movement of the 1870s, but the real boost came from the publication of an annotated bible by the evangelist Cyrus Scofield in 1909. The *Scofield Reference Bible* became the standard source of exegesis for generations of evangelical Christians, with a number of bible schools and seminaries being established, including the well-known Dallas Theological Seminary set up in 1924.

The essence of Christian Zionism is that Israel is a central part of God's plans for humankind, and that God has given the Jews a dispensation to prepare the way for the Second Coming. At the 'End Days', assumed by many evangelicals to be likely to happen in their lifetime, true believers will be taken into paradise in 'the rapture' while Christ will come to rule on earth for a thousand years after the final battle between good and evil. 'Dispensationalism' or 'dispensation theology' are terms commonly used, implying that the dispensation that God has given to the Jews to re-establish and maintain Israel is an essential part of God's entire plan. The current strength of Christian Zionism in the United States is difficult to gauge, but the well-known 'Left Behind' series of books – fictionalized treatments of the End Days theme – have sold tens of millions of copies in the past two decades. Evangelical Christianity is embraced by about one in three of the 300 million Americans, and Christian

Zionism is professed by between a quarter and a third of evangelicals. This is very much larger than the Jewish community in the United States and Christian evangelicals are every bit as supportive of the modern Israel. Moreover, most evangelical Christians in the United States will see Israel as being particularly significant, even if they do not embrace the full implications of Christian Zionism.[9]

On its own, Christian Zionism might be little more than a particular religious trend, except that four aspects of its evolution make it highly relevant in terms of the development of the war on terror. The first is that it has been greatly strengthened by the development of the State of Israel. The founding of the state in the late 1940s was itself significant and was seen as a prophetic phenomenon, in that Jews were beginning to fulfil God's will as expressed in the Scofield Bible and other Christian Zionist writings. This was greatly strengthened by the 1967 Six Day War when Israel extended its boundaries to include Judea, Samaria and Sinai. This went much further in recreating biblical Israel and was widely seen as a sign that the End Days might be approaching. In such circumstances, support for Israel was to become a central part of the outlook of devout Christian Zionists.

The second aspect is the remarkable way in which the Israel lobby in the United States, especially AIPAC, has made common cause with Christian Zionist groups such as the 'International Christian Embassy Jerusalem' and 'Stand for Israel.'[10] This has been a hugely welcome and significant development, given the divisions which have developed in recent years within the American Jewish community over support for Israel. AIPAC's extension of its work with Christian Zionists was particularly necessary during the Clinton years of the mid-1990s, partly because of various preacher scandals in the United States but also because the Clinton administration tended to work more with secular elements of the Israeli political system. Indirectly, AIPAC was also aided at this time by the intense dislike of Clinton by many evangelicals as a result of his questionable sexual activities.

Thirdly, patterns of voting behaviour in the United States include a strong tendency for evangelical Christians to vote for Republican candidates. Furthermore, they are generally more likely to vote than most other sectors of the population. Given that US presidential elections normally get a turnout of only 50 per cent, this makes the electoral influence of evangelical Christians, including Christian Zionists, greater than for many other constituencies.

The final and most significant aspect of the influence of Christian Zionism was its developing relationship with the neoconservatives towards the end of the 1990s. Donald Wagner, a theologian and long-term student of Christian Zionism, points to the remarkable coming together of these strands of religious belief and political ideology, quoting the evangelical preacher Jerry Falwell as saying that 'The Bible Belt is Israel's safety net in the United States.' That the neoconservatives and Christian Zionists could make common cause was aided by the entry into the White House of a born-again Christian in January 2001, but this was in the context of major political changes. As Wagner puts it: 'By 2000, a shift had taken place in the Republican Party. It began embracing the doctrines of neoconservative ideologues who advocated US unilateralism and favoured military solutions over diplomacy. The more aggressive approach was put into action after September 11, and to no-one's surprise, Israel's war against Palestine and its other enemies was soon linked to the US "war on terrorism".'[11]

The unlikely fusion of religious belief and political ideology is largely unrecognized in the political science community. On its own, it might have had some limited influence on the evolution of US–Israel relations, but its impact after 9/11 was to be very much more substantial.

Ending the Saddam Hussein regime

To the surprise of many commentators, the termination of the Saddam Hussein regime in Iraq was to become a major feature of the war on terror within a few months of the 9/11 attacks (see chapter 5), yet there were very clear indications of a deep-rooted antagonism to the regime that pre-date not just the 9/11 attacks but also the election of George W. Bush in November 2000. After the 1991 Gulf War, the administration of President George H. W. Bush had expected the regime to collapse within weeks, but this did not happen and the Bush administration then moved to a policy of active containment. The main features were a rigorous UN and International Atomic Energy Agency inspection process designed to dismantle Iraqi programmes of weapons of mass destruction, together with the early implementation of two 'no-fly' zones covering the Kurdish north and the Shi'a south of Iraq. These were intended to limit the regime's ability to suppress these populations, but a third element was the use of economic sanctions which might further weaken the regime.[12]

Clinton's election in 1992 resulted in a continuation of this containment policy, although there were numerous occasions during the 1990s when military action was taken in pursuit of the no-fly policy, including a major four-day operation, Desert Fox, at the end of 1998. Overall, the Clinton administration characterized containment as a success, and certainly preferable to a major military campaign to terminate the regime. It could point to the successful dismantling of Iraq's nuclear weapons programme in the early 1990s, and the uncovering by UN Special Commission on Iraq inspectors of the extent of the chemical and biological weapons programme in 1995. Furthermore, the Saddam Hussein regime was economically crippled and had little opportunity for developing its military forces. There were enduring controversies over the effects of the sanctions process on the ordinary people of Iraq, not least the increase in child malnutrition, but these criticisms were not sufficient to move the Clinton administration away from its stance.

Towards the end of Clinton's second term, with Iraq hindering the work of the inspectors, the administration became notably more concerned about the status of Iraq's WMD programme, seeing the country as an increasing threat to US regional interests. It was best summed up by Edward Walker, Assistant Secretary of State at the Bureau of Near Eastern Affairs, in March 2000:

> Iraq under Saddam Hussein remains dangerous, unreconstructed and defiant. Saddam's record makes clear that he will remain a threat to regional peace and security as long as he remains in power. He will not relinquish what remains of his WMD arsenal. He will not live in peace with his neighbors. He will not cease the repression of the Iraqi people.[13]

Such a statement has to be understood in the context of a presidential election campaign which, in early 2000, included substantial criticisms of Clinton's Iraq policy, but Walker's use of the phrase, '... what remains of his WMD arsenal', is significant. The implication was that the multilateral process of UN inspections and sanctions had at least weakened the Iraqi WMD programme, even if the country remained a threat.

For Republican critics of the Clinton administration, especially neoconservatives, the Iraq policy was blatant evidence of a much wider failure of Clinton's world-view. What was commonly termed 'liberal internationalism', especially the manner in which US foreign and security policy was constrained by the need to work with the UN, was anathema. It was seen as the most substantial obstacle to the idea of a New American Century where the United States had to play a vibrant and robust leadership role and not be tied down by the concerns of lesser states. One of the leading critics, John

Bolton, was later to take a senior position in the State Department under George Bush. He expressed this intense dislike of the Clinton administration's attitude to Iraq at the time of the brief Desert Fox air assault on Iraq which stopped far short of threatening the survival of the Saddam Hussein regime. Writing in *The Weekly Standard* under the title of 'Our Pitiful Iraq Policy', Bolton said:

> [Clinton's] embarrassing failure in November to punish Iraq militarily illuminates two broad and profoundly disturbing themes of his foreign policy. The first is his near-compulsive unwillingness to use decisive military force to achieve critical American objectives, even when conditions are ideal. The second is his addictive adherence to multilateralism, reflected here in his continued preference for UN weapons inspections over the elimination of Saddam Hussein's regime.[14]

Bolton was effectively speaking for a wide swathe of Republican opinion at the time, and there was a persistent movement advocating a far tougher policy towards Iraq throughout Clinton's second term. This included a series of proposals for taking direct military action against the regime, although most of these stopped short of a complete occupation of the country. Instead, what was advocated was an extension of the air exclusion zones to include direct military aid, including the possible deployment of US troops on the ground. If the Saddam Hussein regime was physically excluded from southern Iraq, for example, a provisional government could be established which could use the huge wealth of the southern oilfields both to starve the Saddam Hussein heartland of revenues and develop the beginnings of a new Iraq. This would ultimately lead to the collapse of the regime and its replacement with a new government that would be closely allied to the United States. Not only would a dangerous regime be eliminated but a new pro-American Iraq would be an impressive counter to the influence of Iran.

At a more formal level, opposition to Clinton's Iraq stance was expressed through numerous debates in Congress, together with a series of well-publicized letters sent to the administration or to the Congressional leadership. The persistent theme was the elimination of the Saddam Hussein regime and, when Bush was elected in November 2000, there was a confident expectation of a change of policy. Initially there were few indications that this would happen. Although, as already mentioned, there were many other examples of unilateral action in the early months of 2001, on the issue of Iraq the new administration simply began a series of discussions to formulate policy.

This was partly a reflection of the appointment of Colin Powell as Secretary of State since Powell, with his extensive military experience, was not convinced of the viability of regime termination by military action. His own preference was for 'containment plus' through 'smart' sanctions, an approach that was received badly in neoconservative circles. However, given Powell's status as a hugely experienced wartime general, there were limits to the extent of such criticisms in public. Behind the scenes, though, the summer of 2001 was a period of substantial disagreement, with neoconservatives and others remaining adamant that the Saddam Hussein regime had to be terminated.

Conclusion

The late 1990s had been a period in US politics when powerful interest groups had promoted the vision of a New American Century that was about to unfold. With the election of George W. Bush in November 2000, an administration was formed that embraced a more unilateralist approach, especially on issues of international security. By the late summer of 2001, there was a conviction that this was not only the correct approach but that it was working, as US international leadership became more evident. Given the power of the United States in what was now a unipolar world, it had a responsibility for leadership that was held in some political circles with an almost religious intensity. There was a clear duty to lead and, in leading, the security of the United States would be assured. What was good for the White House was necessarily good for the world.

With specific reference to the Middle East, two other political issues were relevant in analysing the response to the 9/11 attacks. One was the level of support for Israel, stemming not just from the traditional Jewish lobby but also from the rise to political influence of the Christian Zionism movement. The second was the strong commitment to regime termination in Iraq that stretched across most of the Republican Party.

In examining the US response to 9/11, though, it is essential to go well beyond the immediate political context in two distinct respects which will be covered in the next two chapters. One is to examine the military context, especially in terms of the evolution of the US armed forces after the end of the Cold War and some key aspects of their experience in the 1991 war with Iraq. The other is to analyse the growing significance of oil security for the United States, especially the changing attitudes to the immense oil reserves of the Persian Gulf region. This is an issue that has grown substantially in importance since the 1970s and has its origins some thirty years earlier. It is an aspect of the US security outlook that has received surprisingly little coverage in the international relations literature but is essential to understanding US policy in the region since 9/11.

CHAPTER TWO

The US Military Posture

Introduction

Chapter 1 examined the political context for the war on terror that followed the 9/11 attacks. While it covered the political developments that did much to determine the uncompromising nature of the US response to the attacks, that response was also dictated by the nature and recent evolution of US military forces. These had changed substantially since the ending of the Cold War at the close of the 1980s, especially as forces that had evolved in the context of a perceived global threat from the Soviet Union were transformed into a military capability to 'keep the violent peace' wherever that might be at risk across the world.

The nature and extent of US military forces in 2001 gave the Bush administration particular capabilities, some of which hardly existed in 1990. Moreover, two further factors were particularly relevant. One was the experience of the 1991 Gulf War and the other was an enduring if little recognized US concern with oil security in general, and with the security of Persian Gulf oil supplies in particular. While these features were relevant to the immediate responses to 9/11 in Afghanistan and across Central Asia, they were to become very much more relevant in understanding the extension of the war on terror to Iraq and, potentially, Iran.

Force transformation

When President Clinton's first Director of Central Intelligence, James Woolsey, appeared before a Senate committee in
1993 to confirm his appointment, he was asked to characterize
the change in international security from the Cold War to the
post-Cold War world. He said that the United States had slain
the dragon but now lived in a jungle full of poisonous snakes.[1]
This expression neatly summarizes the changed outlook in the
Pentagon as US forces made the transition to a less certain
world in which a clear-cut confrontation with another superpower in a bipolar world was replaced by far less predictable
threats from diverse sources.

Shortly after the Berlin Wall had come down in 1989 and it
became obvious that the Soviet bloc was imploding, there were
expressions of hope of a 'new world order' in which the intensity
of confrontation would be replaced by relative peace. By 1994,
the Iraq War and evolving conflicts in the Balkans, the Caucasus
and the Great Lakes region of Eastern Africa had rendered that
implausibly optimistic, with the Iraq War having been a particular shock. In seeing the need to 'tame the jungle', the US armed
forces then underwent a progressive transformation, as did the
armed forces of countries such as the UK and France.

Although there were decreases in overall defence spending,
they turned out to be far removed from the anticipated peace
dividend that might have been expected to follow the ending of
the Cold War. Analysts could point to a substantial cutback in
world military expenditure in the early 1990s, but this was very
largely due to the collapse of defence budgets in Russia and the
other former Soviet states. For the United States and its allies, it
was much more of a transformation rather than a draw-down.

For the US military, the changes mainly fell into three cat-
egories – changes in force disposition, decreasing numbers of
military personnel and increased reliance on technologies.

In terms of force disposition, the most significant involved nuclear forces, heavy armour and anti-submarine weaponry. Strategic nuclear forces were cut back substantially, mainly by agreement with Russia, and tactical nuclear forces were very largely withdrawn, mainly through unilateral moves. While the United States remained a very substantial nuclear power, with thousands of weapons deployed and many thousands more in reserve, the overall force levels were very much lower than the 20,000-plus warhead numbers of the Cold War era.[2] Similarly, the large numbers of main battle tanks and other heavily armoured military vehicles that were based principally in West Germany in earlier decades were cut back severely, just as the US Navy decreased its anti-submarine forces. In the 1980s there had been much talk of the need for a 600-ship navy as being the optimum force to constrain the Soviet Union. That was never achieved and, by the mid-1990s, a 400-ship navy seemed more likely.

In general terms, the numbers of serving military declined by around a quarter during the 1990s, but this disguised a major change in the overall configuration. While the US Navy, for example, cut its anti-submarine forces substantially, it very largely maintained its force of aircraft carriers and its ability to deploy them in multi-ship carrier battle groups. Thus its expeditionary potential remained largely intact. The US Air Force moved away from a very large measure of overseas basing, especially in Western Europe and the West Pacific, but maintained its ability to undertake air strikes anywhere in the world at short notice, using strategic bombers such as the B-52, the B-1 and the stealthy B-2. Moreover, it configured many of its forces into Air Expeditionary Wings, which were effectively sizeable integrated air forces that could deploy readily to standby bases in strategic locations overseas.

The US Army suffered the largest cuts in personnel but put more emphasis on Special Forces and on the ability to deploy forces such as the 82nd Airborne Division rapidly. Perhaps the most interesting development was in the make-up of the US Marine Corps. During the Cold War and within the US military, the Marine Corps was a separate branch of the armed forces that numbered close to 200,000 personnel, making it larger than the entire armies of most European countries, including Britain. The Corps had developed slowly during the early twentieth century, with numerous actions across Latin America in support of US interests, and had then become a much larger entity during the Pacific War against the Japanese. In the subsequent Cold War period, the Marine Corps was seen as having a key role in constraining the Soviet Union around its margins but it was therefore vulnerable to severe cuts once the Cold War had ended.

Instead, the Marine Corps could argue strongly that it was that aspect of US military power that was most practised in the 'taming of jungles', with its expeditionary capabilities and its highly adaptive ships and equipment. This argument was so effective that the Marine Corps maintained almost all its numbers through the 1990s, becoming proportionately more powerful within the US armed forces.

The final development in the 1990s was less transformative than evolutionary, this being the increased reliance on a range of new technologies. This included further improvements in remote sensing through satellite and other electronic observation, the development of early generations of unmanned aerial vehicles (UAVs), the further development of anti-personnel area-impact munitions such as the multi-launch rocket system (MLRS) and, in particular, the deployment of a wide range of precision-guided munitions and stand-off weapons.

This last development was particularly significant in that it gave rise, especially during the 1991 Gulf War, to the idea of 'war against real estate', the ability to destroy material targets while greatly limiting human casualties. This gave the appearance of a kinder or more humane war, but disguised the parallel evolution of area-impact munitions that were specifically designed to kill and maim over the widest area. Including cluster bombs and fuel–air explosives as well as multiple launch rocket systems, these attracted little public attention while having the potential to substantially increase the human costs of conflict.

One major political advantage of new weapons, especially stand-off systems such as air and sea-launched cruise missiles, was that they had the prospect of decreasing casualties within the US military. This was an important response to the 'body bag' syndrome, the reluctance of the US public to accept high military casualties in wars fought overseas. This had been particularly evident at the time of the 'Black Hawk down' episode during US intervention in Mogadishu in 1993 when the deaths of 18 Special Forces resulted in the rapid withdrawal of US troops from Somalia.

The Maritime Strategy

One particular element of the Cold War force posture was especially significant – the development of what became known as the Maritime Strategy.[3] During the Reagan era in the early 1980s, US defence budgets rose quite sharply and the overall force posture towards the Soviet Union became more robust. Much attention was focused on new nuclear systems, including the strategic M-X intercontinental ballistic missile, the new intermediate range systems such as the ground-launched cruise missile and the Pershing 2 ballistic missile, and the moves towards missile defence, popularly known as Star Wars. While these all attracted much attention, not least in Western Europe, they receded in importance as the Cold War wound down at the end of the 1980s.

This was not the case with the Maritime Strategy, which was essentially a US Navy–Marine Corps strategy of developing forces that could take the war to the Soviet mainland in the event of a global confrontation. The thinking here was that a substantive east–west war might be centred primarily on Central and Western Europe, but the superior naval and Marine Corps power of the United States would give it the ability to engage Soviet forces in East Asia and probably the Middle East, diverting Soviet military resources from Europe, and even acquiring territorial gains that might have a considerable value in any negotiated end to conflict.

The Maritime Strategy was developed in the early 1980s, was made public in 1986 and, in its most developed form, was concerned with how the Navy and Marine Corps would function in all-out war with the Soviet Union. Assuming that the conflict, however widespread, fell short of a central nuclear exchange, the strategy envisaged three phases of conflict. First would be a *transition to war* which would involve the mobilization and forward deployment of forces, and this would be followed by *seizing the initiative,* which would concentrate on destroying the ballistic missile submarines of the Soviet nuclear triad, containing other Soviet naval forces and preserving US lines of communication. The final phase, *carrying the war to the enemy*, was described by the then Chief of Naval Operations, Admiral James D. Watkins, in 1986:

> the US and its allies would press home the initiative worldwide, while continuing to support air and land campaigns, maintaining sealift, and keeping sea lines of communication open. Amphibious forces, up to the size of a full Marine Amphibious Force [around 50,000 troops], would be used to regain territory. In addition, the full weight of the carrier battle forces could continue to 'roll up' the Soviets on the flanks, contribute to the battle on the Central Front, or carry the war to the Soviets.[4]

While the development of this strategy was primarily directed at the Soviet Union, it resulted during the Reagan administration of the early 1980s in a worldwide increase in military readiness. As Watkins put it, again in 1986: 'We now maintain a continual presence in the Indian Ocean, Persian Gulf and Caribbean, as well as our more traditional forward deployments to the Mediterranean and Western Pacific. Although we are not at war today, our operating tempo has been about 20 percent higher than during the Vietnam War.'[5]

To support the Maritime Strategy, there was a major programme of enhancing global reach, including the build-up of bases such as Diego Garcia in the Indian Ocean and Guam in the West Pacific, with a particular emphasis on maritime prepositioning and on the ability to move large quantities of combat-related material. Fleets of specialized ships were deployed to support the Marine Corps and even Second World War battleships of the *Iowa* class were brought back from reserve to serve as support for coastal operations.

While the Maritime Strategy was somewhat scaled down towards the end of the 1980s, the 1990–1 Gulf War involved a heavy reliance on Navy and Marine Corps facilities and further emphasized the importance of the Persian Gulf. During the 1990s, therefore, the culture within the Navy and the Marine Corps remained very much one of global operations, maintaining an operational tempo that was not much less than at the height of the Cold War. The political significance of this was that it gave the United States an unrivalled ability to project power in virtually any part of the world, an ability that was still very much in evidence, and central to Navy and Marine Corps thinking, in September 2001.

Implications of the Gulf War

After the Iraqi invasion of Kuwait in 1990, the United States led a major international coalition against Iraq, with the subsequent war in January–March 1991 involving large contingents from Egypt, Syria and Saudi Arabia, as well as many NATO states. The war was relatively quick and was seen as an almost complete victory for the coalition, even though the Saddam Hussein regime survived in sufficient strength to put down rebellions in the months that followed in the Shi'a south and the Kurdish north-east.

Even so, there were three features of the war that are highly relevant to the more recent 'war on terror': US involvement in Saudi Arabia, the impact of the Iraqi Scud missile launches and Iraq's chemical and biological weapons programmes. The first related to the maintenance of substantial numbers of US military personnel in Saudi Arabia, especially major air force units at Dhahran, after the end of the Gulf War. During the course of the 1990s, this provided an increasingly potent focus for radical Islamists, especially those associated with what later became termed the al-Qaida movement. For them, the presence of foreign forces, especially from the United States, in the Kingdom of the Two Holy Places, was entirely unacceptable and was to be opposed with at least the intensity with which the Soviet Union had been evicted from Afghanistan during the 1980s. While not regarded as particularly significant until the late 1990s, this aspect of US involvement in Saudi Arabia was to become highly relevant after 9/11.

Scuds and Star Wars

The second issue concerned the impact of Iraq's Scud missiles. The Gulf War started late on 16 January 1991 with a substantial series of air raids conducted from airbases across the region and from aircraft carriers at sea. Sea-launched cruise missiles were also used and the opening attacks of the war even utilized B-52 strategic bombers armed with air-launched cruise missiles and operating from the continental United States. The massive air raids were reported across the world in a manner that suggested a very short war with high levels of confidence that the comprehensive destruction of Iraq's air force, air defences, command and control systems and logistic support would all lead rapidly to a brief ground campaign that would evict the Iraqis from Kuwait.

Within twenty-four hours, the situation had changed dramatically as the first Iraqi Scud missiles landed in Israel. The physical damage was minimal but the psychological impact and the political consequences were potentially immense. Given the unpredictability of the Scud attacks and the lack of effective missile defences, the Israeli government immediately faced a population exposed to a degree of uncertainty and fear that had not been experienced since the early days of the Yom Kippur–Ramadan War of October 1973. The United States therefore faced the possibility of Israel retaliating against Iraq, the consequences of which would be disastrous for Washington since it would probably lead to a withdrawal of key Arab forces, especially those from Egypt. This, in turn, would lead to a fracturing of the coalition and would give the very strong impression of an attack on Iraq being a US–Israeli action against an Arab state. This may well have been the main motive in the Saddam Hussein regime attacking Israel in the first place.

In order to avoid this, the coalition put a massive effort into a hunt for the mobile Scud launchers deployed in western Iraq, using a combination of air power and Special Forces. Furthermore, the United States airlifted Patriot anti-aircraft missile batteries to Israel as these had some limited defensive potential against the Scud missiles. The Scuds themselves, and an extended range Iraqi-produced version, the al-Hussein, were essentially 1950s' technology of very limited accuracy, but their political impact was considerable, serving as a reminder to the US military that such systems could, in certain circumstances, be deeply problematic. In the immediate circumstances of the Iraq War, the 'Scud hunt' resulted in a delay of around three weeks in the start of the ground war, a significant change in what was essentially a six-week conflict.

In addition to the attacks on Israel, numerous missiles were also fired at major military concentrations in eastern Saudi Arabia. In spite of their inaccuracy, one of them caused the worst single loss to US forces throughout the war when it destroyed a storage and billeting depot in Dhahran on 25 February, killing 28 people. While this was of immediate and longer-term concern for the US military authorities, it became apparent long after the war that another incident had had even greater implications.

Although there had been some pre-positioning of supplies and equipment in Saudi Arabia during the 1980s, especially the building of airbases that were very much larger than required by the Royal Saudi Air Force, the actual military operation against Iraq was undertaken primarily through a massive air- and sealift operation, supporting over 500,000 personnel. This involved the use of the large commercial ports on the Persian Gulf and Red Sea coasts of Saudi Arabia, one of the most important being the Red Sea port of Al Jubayl. On 16 February 1991, a few days before the Dhahran attack, a Scud missile aimed at Al Jubayl landed in the sea just 300 yards from the US Navy's aviation support ship *Wright* and close to the amphibious warfare ship *Tarawa*. The two ships, along with other war-related vessels, were moored alongside a large pier complex that also included a large ammunition storage dump and a parking area for gasoline tankers. No damage was sustained but had the Scud hit the complex and set off a chain of explosions the effects would have been disastrous.[6]

The experience of the Scud attacks, both on Israel and on US facilities in Saudi Arabia, had a substantial effect on US military thinking. Although the Saddam Hussein regime had built up substantial armed forces, the reality was that the great majority of these were poorly trained conscripts who might have been relevant to the stalemate of the long war against Iran in the 1980s, but had little prospect of resisting the massive international coalition established by the United States and its coalition partners. Moreover, Iraq faced an antagonistic Iran to its east, Arab states including Syria, Egypt and Saudi Arabia to the west and south, and Turkey to the north. In such circumstances it was in a position of weakness. Even so, the use of a singularly crude missile technology had altered the course of the war and had had a substantial political effect. This was an unexpected outcome, whatever the sense of victory at the end of the war, and it gave the US military considerable pause for thought. If a state such as Iraq could utilize such weapons so effectively, there was a strong possibility that future US regional operations in pursuit of its security interests could be substantially limited.

A major effect of the Scud incidents, along with a more general concern over missile proliferation in countries such as North Korea, was a rethink of attitudes to missile defence in the 1990s, with a renewed emphasis on defences geared to particular regional theatres. The US Navy was particularly prominent in this, seeking to modify existing missiles and radar systems to meet this perceived threat, and the US Army worked to upgrade its Patriot system into the PAC 3 (Patriot Advanced Capability). Meanwhile, the US Air Force commenced the development of a hugely innovative system, the world's first powerful directed energy weapon, the Airborne Laser.[7] All in all, this legacy of the Gulf War was to influence military developments for more than a decade, but had an added impact because of one further aspect of the war, the Iraqi programme to develop chemical and biological weapons.

Iraqi chemical and biological weapons

In the 1970s, the increasingly repressive Ba'ath Party in Iraq invested heavily in both civil and military developments, boosted by the substantial oil price rises of 1973–4. From a Baghdad perspective, Iraq might have had a much smaller population than regional powers such as Iran, Turkey and Egypt but it had a determined and single-minded government that saw the opportunity for a regional power base, especially as Iran was beginning to experience internal political upheavals towards the end of the decade. Even so, Iran was believed to be in the early stages of developing a nuclear weapons programme and Israel was already a significant nuclear power. In such circumstances, the Ba'ath regime saw a requirement for developing its own weapons of mass destruction with early work on chemical and nuclear weapons getting under way in the late 1970s.

As an initial step towards developing a plutonium-based nuclear weapon, the Osiraq research reactor that was developed with French aid was not hugely significant but it was an indication of intentions and would also provide substantial training and research opportunities for a nuclear weapons programme. By the beginning of the 1980s, the Iranian Revolution had resulted in massive upheavals and the Saddam Hussein regime instigated the Iran–Iraq War, primarily to gain territory and influence in western Iran. The chaos of the Revolution largely removed any early prospect of Iran developing nuclear weapons but Iraq's potential in this direction was sufficient for the Israelis to destroy the Osiraq reactor in an air raid in 1981.

While Israel considered this operation an outstanding success, the reality was that Iraq then proceeded to take the much more dispersed and robust uranium route to nuclear weapons and also reinforced its chemical weapons development programme, using chemical weapons repeatedly in the later years of the Iran–Iraq War, both against Iranian troops and against its own Iraqi Kurdish population. Furthermore, the Saddam Hussein regime took the important step in 1985 of starting a major programme to develop offensive biological systems. By the end of the 1980s, numerous biological agents had been researched and tested. Some of them were lethal to humans, others were severely incapacitating and yet others were intended for use against crops, causing indirect economic damage. The biological warfare programme extended to developing the technologies to deploy and deliver active biological agents by means of aircraft spray tanks and medium-range ballistic missiles.

Of the many biological agents studied, three received the most attention, *Clostridium botulinum*, the micro-organism producing the botulinum toxin, *Bacillus anthracis*, which causes anthrax, and species of the *Aspergillus* fungus that produce a carcinogenic toxin – aflatoxin. Large-scale production of anthrax spores and botulinum toxin commenced in 1989, with one facility alone producing 6,000 litres of concentrated botulinum toxin and 8,425 litres of anthrax. Other organisms studied included a rotavirus that caused severe diarrhoea and a virus causing haemorrhagic conjunctivitis, an acute eye condition that causes temporary blindness and great pain, with an intensely debilitating effect on victims.

From 1988 to 1990, a programme that paralleled the production of biological warfare agents was concerned with weaponizing them, and this was greatly expanded when the coalition responded to the Iraqi invasion of Kuwait with a huge build-up of forces intended to provide the means to defeat the Iraqi forces and expel them from Kuwait. During the key period from August 1990 through to the outbreak of the 1991 war, weaponization was completed to the extent that Iraq then had 166 bombs ready for use, 50 filled with anthrax, 100 with botulinum toxin and 16 with aflatoxin. Furthermore, an urgent programme to develop missile warheads was also implemented, with 25 al-Hussein missiles ready for deployment by January 1991, 13 with botulinum warheads, 10 with anthrax and two with aflatoxin.[8]

Almost all of this information later came into the public domain through the work of the inspectors of the UN Special Commission on Iraq in the mid-1990s after the war, but the general features were known to western intelligence agencies prior to the war. Indeed a US inter-agency National Intelligence Estimate of November 1990 indicated that Iraq had such systems and would be prepared to use them *in extremis* if the regime were facing destruction.[9] What was particularly significant in the findings of UNSCOM was that the biological weapons – spray bombs and missiles – were deployed to four bases immediately before the start of the 1991 war, with orders pre-delegated to local commanders to use the weapons against coalition forces should Baghdad be destroyed.

Although not certain, it is probable that the regime was anticipating an Israeli response to the Scud attacks leading to an escalation of the conflict and the possibility that the coalition, with or without Israeli involvement, would decide on regime termination. Given that Iraq had used chemical weapons in the earlier war with Iran, escalation to battlefield CW use was possible in the chaotic conditions of war, raising the potential for nuclear retaliation from the United States. Such a scenario seems far-fetched but this was a conflict that was certainly capable of escalation and in which Iraq had chemical weapons and the United States had nuclear weapons, with Israel an entirely uncertain factor.

Two further points should be considered. One is that the Iraqi BW deployment decision may have been primarily one of deterring the United States and its coalition partners from going beyond the immediate war aim of evicting Iraqi forces from Basra to encompass regime termination by military occupation. For such deterrence to work, the US military authorities would have had to have known about the BW deployment plan, but as indicated above, the National Intelligence Estimate just before the war does suggest just that.

Secondly, it is by no means clear that all of the BW systems would have worked. BW spray bombs involve only reasonably sophisticated technology but producing missile warheads that can survive the heat of re-entry and successfully disperse a live agent such as anthrax is much more difficult. It is not at all certain that the Iraqis had succeeded in such a task. At the same time, this is not a fundamental issue since it would have been routine for the US intelligence analysts to assume that the Iraqis had this capability in the absence of direct evidence to the contrary. Risks could not be taken.

Gulf War aftermath

Putting together these three issues relating to the Gulf War – US military forces in Saudi Arabia, the Scud missiles and the Iraqi CBW programme – we get both an appreciation of the effect of the war on US military thinking and also an indication of the political circumstances in Saudi Arabia that aided the subsequent development of the al-Qaida movement. The implications of the Scud experience and of the potential risk from Iraqi CBW were that a relatively middle-ranking power such as Iraq had the capability to engage in what amounted to asymmetric warfare in a manner that severely constrained the United States and its coalition partners. Most of the analyses published in the months and years that followed pointed to a startlingly successful campaign that achieved the result of a comprehensive eviction of Iraqi forces from Kuwait, with very low casualties for the coalition, whatever the military and civilian costs to the Iraqis.

In one sense this was correct in that the Saddam Hussein regime was indeed humiliated, but the Scud and CBW experiences were illuminating for the US military in that both resulted in considerable limitations for the conduct of the war. The 'Scud hunt' was a major diversion and the CBW risk was one reason for not proceeding beyond the eviction of the Iraqi forces from Kuwait towards regime termination. In the immediate euphoria of victory, especially after only 100 hours of ground war, there was an assumption that the Saddam Hussein regime was finished, with its likely survival time measured in weeks rather than months. It came as a major surprise that the regime survived not just the defeat itself and its economic and social aftermath, but was able to consolidate its forces in order to suppress uprisings in the Shi'a south and the Kurdish north, so much so that international public opinion forced coalition states to erect northern and southern no-fly zones to limit Iraqi air activity in pursuit of rebel groups.

The third factor – the stationing of US forces in Saudi Arabia after the war – became significant during the 1990s as the al-Qaida movement developed its power base. For convinced jihadists, a profound motive for fighting Soviet forces in Afghanistan in the 1980s had been the intense desire to evict occupying forces from an essentially Islamic state. For such people, the basing of US forces in the Kingdom of the Two Holy Places was a far greater affront, and did much to increase support for Osama bin Laden and his followers, even if most of their activities in the latter part of the decade were directed back in Afghanistan. There, their Taliban allies were still attempting to complete their control of the country in the closing stages of the civil war with the Northern Alliance (see chapter 6).

Meanwhile, in Saudi Arabia, there were three developments during the 1990s that were to become significant in explaining the later extension of the war on terror to Iraq. One was the growth of radical jihadist groups such as al-Qaida within Saudi Arabia as a result of a process of marginalization. During the late 1970s and early 1980s, high oil prices ensured a very high flow of revenues into the Kingdom, with rapid economic development across most sectors of the economy, including heavy investment in education. While many of the more technically orientated and professional jobs went to expatriates, by the early 1990s, many tens of thousands of young Saudi men were entering the job market from high schools and technical colleges each year. By then, though, the job market had shrunk as the economy faltered in an era of lower oil prices, leaving large numbers of young men unemployed and on the margins, unless they had connections with one of the 'thousand princely families'. Inevitably this resulted in a deepening antagonism to the House of Saud and an increase in support for radical alternatives, including movements such as al-Qaida.

The second development was a series of attacks on US military facilities in Saudi Arabia. This started with small-scale and relatively isolated attacks on US soldiers in the early 1990s but attained a far more dangerous level with an attack on an accommodation block at the major airbase at Dhahran in eastern Saudi Arabia. On 25 June 1996, a sewage disposal tanker containing a large explosive charge was placed in front of the Khobar Towers block of flats. When it detonated, the whole of the front of the tower block collapsed, injuring around 500 people and killing 19 Americans. Coming after the earlier attacks, this was something of a nightmare for US military forces in Saudi Arabia, indicating that the country was no longer a safe location. The problem was that those responsible for the various attacks were not clearly defined enemy forces from a named state, even if some US investigators later blamed Iran for an involvement in the Khobar Towers attack. Instead, the United States faced radical groups prepared to use paramilitary tactics in a largely unpredictable fashion.

The US Air Force's response to the Khobar Towers attack was to review its overall security in the Kingdom, the result being the decision to move the main air force facilities from Dhahran to a new base in a remote location in the desert south of Riyadh in the centre of Saudi Arabia. The Prince Sultan Air Force Base was rapidly constructed after 1996 using a standby facility already available, and within two years the most important force available in the region, squadrons equipped with the F-15E Strike Eagle aircraft, was securely located at Prince Sultan. In addition to its location, the airbase had very high levels of perimeter security, with around 400 of the 4,000 personnel at the base being entirely concerned with that security.[10]

The third development in Saudi Arabia related directly to both of the trends just outlined. For the House of Saud, the rise of jihadist movements antagonistic to the royal family and to US forces in the Kingdom was a considerable worry, mitigated partly by the relocation of the largest US military base away from the urban areas of eastern Saudi Arabia to an interior location. This may have eased matters but it was not enough to satisfy the Saudi authorities when a major crisis developed at the end of 1998, a crisis that had a profound effect on US military attitudes to the Kingdom and helped provide a particularly strong motive for terminating the Saddam Hussein regime five years later.

During the course of the 1990s, there had been periodic confrontations with the Saddam Hussein regime, including repeated air actions designed to enforce the no-fly zone. On occasions these extended to cruise missile attacks on targets in Baghdad, but tensions escalated in the latter months of 1998, ostensibly in relation to particular Iraqi infringements of the no-fly zones. It is possible that US intelligence agencies were linked to an intended coup attempt against the Saddam Hussein regime, but the end result was a substantial series of air raids over a four-day period in December 1998 known as Operation Desert Fox. British air units were involved but the primary forces were drawn from the US Air Force and carrier-based strike aircraft of the US Navy.

Perhaps the most important components of Desert Fox were to be the F-15E aircraft based at Prince Sultan. The F-15E was a version of the F-15 that had been developed specifically in the medium-range strike role, carrying a range of precision-guided munitions and originally conceived as a powerful addition to US forces in Europe in the closing stages of the Cold War some ten years previously. With appropriate modifications and training, it was the key aircraft available in the region for air operations against targets in Iraq, with the units at Prince Sultan specifically and intensively trained for such operations. Prince Sultan was, in essence, the key to Desert Fox. It was therefore a considerable limitation for the US military when the Saudi authorities refused to allow the United States to use any facilities in the Kingdom base for direct offensive operations against Iraq. Backup activities such as reconnaissance or the air defence of the Kingdom were acceptable, but not strike operations against Iraq. In spite of a marked antagonism towards the Saddam Hussein regime, the assessment within the Kingdom was that for foreign forces to stage an attack on a neighbouring Arab state was potentially destabilizing, providing a further motive for improved jihadist recruitment.[11]

This refusal was a matter of substantial concern in Washington, but an added factor emerged. Not only was the US Air Force refused permission to fly offensive missions over Iraq, but the Saudi authorities also refused to allow the USAF to redeploy the key force of F-15E strike aircraft to neighbouring countries such as Kuwait that might be willing to host them. While Desert Fox went ahead, it was a more limited operation and ended within four days with little direct impact on the Saddam Hussein regime. In the aftermath of this experience, the reliability of the House of Saud in times of regional crisis was called into question, bearing in mind its concern with internal security. This meant that in the wider Persian Gulf region by the end of the 1990s, the United States faced an uncontrolled Saddam Hussein regime in Iraq, an oppositional Islamic Republic of Iran, and the Kingdom of Saudi Arabia in which there were now distinct risks of instability that had already limited US freedom of action.

Conclusion

The response of the Bush administration to the 9/11 attacks was partly dependent on the nature and abilities of the US armed forces. This chapter has analysed the changes in the US military in the decade after the end of the Cold War, demonstrating that cutbacks in forces were primarily directed at those aspects relevant to the previous confrontation with the Soviet Union. Other aspects of the US force posture were maintained and, in some cases, enhanced with particular features relevant to the experience of the 1991 war. The ability to project military force had been a major feature of the Cold War years and the Maritime Strategy, in particular, was very much about 'taking the war' to the Soviet Union. Most of that capability survived, even if it was now directed more to a disparate and not entirely predictable global environment. In one sense, what remained was no longer counterbalanced by Soviet capabilities and therefore gave the United States an extraordinarily strong military capability, supporting its status as the sole superpower. The jungle might need a substantial amount of taming but the United States, and to a certain extent its allies, would be well up to the task. The control paradigm was extant.

Furthermore, one interesting question arises out of the experience of the 1990s in the context of the 1991 Gulf War.

After that war, US forces consolidated their position in Saudi Arabia, especially at major bases such as Dhahran and later, as we have seen, at the Prince Sultan Airbase south of Riyadh. Yet before the war, there was virtually no uniformed US military presence in the Kingdom. Somehow, though, an immensely strong international force of around 600,000 troops and over 1,000 planes was able to assemble in Saudi Arabia in a few short months, from mid-August to December 1990, and was then able to conduct massive military operations against the Iraqi forces in Kuwait, together with an air war across much of Iraq as a whole.

It is worth asking how this was possible. Ordinarily, to transport and assemble such a force would greatly overwhelm the facilities of a host country such as Saudi Arabia. If air forces that were six or more times the size of the Royal Saudi Air Force were deployed without the time to build new facilities, they would greatly exceed the capacity of the RSAF's existing airbases to cope. Similarly, ground forces numbering several hundred thousand troops would require an extraordinary logistics chain as well as the substantial rudiments of basing facilities. The question therefore is, how was the US-led coalition able to cope? Even though this deals with events close to twenty years ago, the answer is as relevant today as it was then, and concerns the singular importance of the Persian Gulf region in the world oil economy in general, and the oil security of the United States in particular.

CHAPTER THREE

Oil and the War on Terror

Introduction

Before exploring the relationship of the oil issue to the war on terror, one point is worth making. The stated reasons for the US decision to terminate the Saddam Hussein regime in 2003, the presence of weapons of mass destruction and the latter's support for terrorist groups, rapidly proved illusory, if not false. As a result, some commentators have sought explanations in other factors, with one of the presumed motives being the potential for US-orientated transnational oil corporations (TNOCs) to make substantial financial gains from developing Iraqi oil resources following a US occupation. While there may be some truth in this, that is not the argument to be explored here – the specific question of Iraqi oil is not the central issue in appreciating US attitudes to Gulf oil security. Instead, it is necessary to get a much broader perspective that stretches over seventy years. In doing so, the specific question raised about the 1990–1 deployments in Saudi Arabia at the end of the previous chapter can be considered.

US oil dependency

Until the early 1940s, the United States was able to fuel its growing economy almost entirely from domestic energy resources, principally oil and coal, with some natural gas. In the case of the oil industry, the broad historical sequence was

43

of initial discoveries in states such as Pennsylvania and Ohio at the end of the nineteenth century, with subsequent discoveries in Texas, Oklahoma and California, followed in due course by Louisiana.[1] During the middle years of the twentieth century, oil exploration began to move offshore, principally in the Gulf of Mexico but also off the coast of California, and this was followed by the proving of substantial reserves in Alaska, especially in the 1970s.

An overall pattern emerged of adequate reserves to meet requirements, right through to the end of the 1960s, although there were two aspects that were relevant to oil dependency even before then. One was that there was a huge acceleration in demand for oil during the Second World War, primarily because of direct military demands in the twin wars in Western Europe and the Pacific, and partly because of the intensity of mass production of wartime material and the parallel economic boom within the United States itself. As a result, even the Roosevelt administration was concerned with oil security, and this was later reflected in early Cold War fears for the stability of the Middle East, especially in the increasingly important Persian Gulf region. Whereas Britain and France had the greater influence in Iraq, Kuwait and Iran, the United States did much to encourage US oil majors to engage in agreements with and investment in Saudi Arabia, as well as working increasingly closely with the Shah of Iran.[2]

The second aspect is that the United States was not entirely self-sufficient in oil, even in the 1960s, but this was a matter primarily of straight economics rather than political strategy. The well-established oil production industry of Venezuela, for example, provided a source of cheap oil of particular qualities, and it was therefore profitable for US oil companies to rely on such supplies, even in the presence of domestically available reserves. Thus in 1960, the United States produced just over 7 million barrels a day (mbd) of oil but had a total consumption of over 9 mbd. This changed little in the following decade, although oil import dependency rose slightly. By 1970, total consumption had risen to 14.8 mbd, of which domestic production provided 9.6 mbd. In the early 1970s there were quite sudden changes as demand for oil rose rapidly while domestic production began to fall. By 1973, consumption had gone up to 16.4 mbd as production slipped to 9.2 mbd. This was of little concern in the United States, given the vigour of the US economy and the low price of oil on world markets.

OPEC and the Yom Kippur–Ramadan War

Largely because of the control of the world oil industry exercised by a handful of oil companies, some oil-producing countries had attempted to form some kind of producer organization with a view to improving prices and taking control of their own oil extraction industries. Venezuela first suggested this in 1949 but that attempt failed. A second attempt in 1960, also prompted by Venezuela, resulted in five countries – Iraq, Iran, Kuwait, Saudi Arabia and Venezuela – agreeing to establish the Organization of Petroleum Exporting Countries (OPEC), with its headquarters in Vienna. During the 1960s, OPEC expanded to include countries such as Indonesia, Ecuador and Nigeria, and a smaller grouping, the Organization of Arab Petroleum Exporting Countries (OAPEC), was also set up.

During that decade, OPEC was singularly unsuccessful in engineering improved conditions and prices for oil exports, yet it did develop a political and economic power base that was largely unrecognized in western countries and among the major oil companies. The changing economic power relationship between producer countries and the oil multinationals was due to a combination of factors. One was the increasing importance of oil as an energy source during the 1960s, especially the growth of the motor industry and the move away from coal for space heating, and a second was the slow-down in the discovery of oil reserves outside the OPEC member states. Furthermore, the power of the seven major TNOCs began to be eroded by the activities of independent oil companies such as the state-owned Total (French) and AGIP (Italian) companies and private companies such as Conoco. Another factor was the systematic effort of several OPEC member states to train their own nationals in oil industry operations. Together with their increasing wealth, these factors gave them a degree of financial and technical resilience. Perhaps most significant was the degree of political unity that OPEC was developing in the early 1970s, in spite of major differences of political organization and regional rivalries.

Even with these evolving advantages, OPEC remained relatively ineffectual, although the Libyan coup of 1969 and the subsequent nationalization of the oil industry in 1973, achieved without a hostile response from oil companies, was an indication of changing relationships. The major change was as substantial as it was unexpected. In late September 1973, complex negotiations between OPEC and the major oil companies were achieving little but were overshadowed by the outbreak of the Yom Kippur–Ramadan War between Israel and Syria and Egypt. This was essentially a sudden and large-scale attempt by Syria and Egypt to regain territory lost to Israel in the 1967 Six Day War. Both states made progress in the early days of the conflict, Syria succeeding in moving heavy armour on to the north-eastern parts of the Golan Heights and Egyptian forces managing to cross the Suez Canal, breach the Bar Lev defensive line and move into parts of western Sinai.

Although the Israeli forces were caught largely by surprise and suffered considerable losses in the early days of intensive fighting, rapid mobilization and the immediate utilization of reserve units and materiel meant that the advances of both the

Syrian and Egyptian forces were halted within a few days of the start of the war. Aid from the United States was immediate, in the form of a large-scale airlift of emergency equipment, especially munitions. While such materiel was not necessarily put into the war immediately, it meant that the Israeli Defence Forces could deplete their own reserves in the knowledge that new supplies were being delivered. This enabled the IDF to operate at a very high level of munitions usage in both theatres of operation. Partly as a result of this, the Syrian forces were held on the Golan Heights and the Egyptians were forced into a retreat.

For Egypt, the situation ten days into the war was becoming dire, with the prospect of Israeli forces crossing to the west of the Suez Canal and even surrounding the Egyptian Third Army. There was therefore the prospect of a second defeat for a major Arab state within six years and it was in these specific circumstances that Arab members of OPEC were prepared to take emergency action designed to persuade western states, and the United States in particular, to use their influence to get an early ceasefire. On 17 September, members of OAPEC met and agreed three measures – a unilateral increase in crude oil prices averaging around 70 per cent, progressive cutbacks in production likely to amount to a 15 per cent decrease in supplies, and an embargo of oil exports to the United States and some European states. This surprising action came at a time of increasing oil prices, mainly through speculation consequent on the effects of the war, but the key factor is that this new price held.

There are arguments as to whether the ceasefire that was agreed a few days later stemmed from this OAPEC action, as other factors may have been involved, including sustained pressure from the Soviet Union, but this is not strictly relevant to this analysis. What is relevant is that the October 1973 action of OAPEC set in motion a much more substantial series of oil price rises in the following months. Some of these were formally agreed OPEC-wide increases, including a near doubling of oil prices in December 1973, and others were unilateral. What was also relevant was that almost all individual oil-producing countries, whether members of OPEC or not, were more than willing to go along with this extraordinary bull market. There was virtually no undercutting, the end result being an overall increase in oil prices between October 1973 and May 1974 of approximately 400 per cent.

A complication for the major consumer states was that this remarkable surge in oil prices was beneficial not just to the producer states but also to the transnational oil companies. This was largely because a common practice for the companies was to raise the price to the end-users, such as motorists at petrol stations, within perhaps twenty days of price rises at source. Given that the supply line from well-head through pipeline, initial processing, maritime transport, refining and storage could be up to 100 days, the profit margins could be exceptional. By and large, the oil companies were able to achieve record profits in 1974.

In general terms, the oil 'shock' of 1973–4 had four different effects. One was to demonstrate that transnational corporations do not necessarily act in the interest of western governments, however close the relationship might normally be. A second was to introduce a period of 'stagflation' in many western economies, as economic stagnation unusually coincided with high levels of inflation. Thirdly, southern states experienced immediate economic downturns leading, among other things, to the 1974 world food crisis and causing them to borrow heavily on international financial markets, a major cause of the third-world debt crisis of the 1980s and 1990s. Finally, the shock had a profound effect in some of the more astute military circles in the United States – the combination of increasing oil import dependency and the ability of oil-producing countries to exercise control over such a key resource was salutary. The United States economy could be subject to a vulnerability that was as unexpected as it was serious.

Oil security and the resource shift

In the wake of the 1973–4 experience, resource analysts within the US Department of Defense recognized two related problems. One was that there were circumstances in which groups of oil-producing states could work together for mutual economic gain. Events such as the Yom Kippur–Ramadan War might be rare, but there were political uncertainties across the Middle East that could lead to local disruptions of supply at any time. The issue here was that if any one country underwent upheavals that limited oil exports, there was no fundamental assurance that other countries would increase production to compensate. In October 1973, after all, they had done the opposite. Furthermore, in extreme circumstances there might even be future occasions when a group of countries such as OAPEC took even stronger action. Such uncertainties were unacceptable.

The second problem was the risk of Soviet involvement in the Persian Gulf region, either in relation to individual oil-rich regimes or even in the event of a full international confrontation between the United States and the Soviet Union that might involve war in the region and an immediate Soviet attempt to take control of Gulf oilfields. Major Soviet intervention in the Middle East was a subsidiary reason for the later development of the US Maritime Strategy described earlier, but it was the potential risk to individual oilfields that exercised minds most strongly in the Pentagon.

The central question was whether the United States had the types of military force that might be required to intervene to secure access to oil supplies. Indeed, this was an issue that even stretched beyond oil supplies to encompass a more general problem of access to strategic resources. As discussed earlier, one of the features of the US oil economy was a growing dependence on imported oil as the domestic fields were slowly depleted. But this was a feature of other US mineral reserves, given that an earlier reliance on domestic reserves of a wide range of ferrous and non-ferrous metal ores was also coming to an end. A number of such metals might not be used in huge quantities, yet they could be essential for a modern industrial economy. In the 1970s, this included cobalt, which had a wide range of electronic uses and was also a constituent of those ferro-cobalt alloys that retained their shape at high temperatures and were therefore essential for rocket motors. Another was tungsten, with its ability to impart hardness at high temperatures in ferro–tungsten alloys, with consequent uses for machine tools. What the United States was experiencing was a phenomenon known as the 'resource shift' which many other industrial economies had earlier experienced in the form of a decreasing availability of domestic resources. Britain, for example, was essentially self-sufficient in coal, iron ore, copper, tin and lead throughout the early part of the industrial revolution, and had developed a primary products trading economy during the latter part of the Victorian era to make up the increasing difference between domestic availability and demand. One reason for the US economic success of the mid-twentieth century was that it was able to rely more on domestic raw materials than any other industrialized state apart from the Soviet Union, but this was coming to an end by the 1970s.

Rapid deployment

Although resource security was a significant issue, almost all the concern after 1973–4 was with oil supplies, with early studies showing that the United States simply did not have the military forces required to move rapidly into areas of potential crisis. This was not for lack of major conventional forces, including the Marine Corps with all its amphibious capability. What was lacking was a combination of two things: rapid deployment and pre-positioning. The United States did not have the means to deploy forces quickly – in days or short weeks rather than long weeks or months – and neither did it have the capability for pre-positioning supplies in regions of anticipated threat and demand.

While most of the analysis of this worrying dimension of national insecurity was limited to classified studies within the Department of Defense, a detailed open-source analysis was undertaken for the Special Subcommittee on Investigations of the House Committee on International Relations. This was undertaken by the Congressional Research Service and was specifically concerned with the nature and extent of the military forces that might be required to take control of foreign oil-fields. Under the heading of 'Oil Fields as Military Objectives', it looked principally at the major oil-producing countries of the Middle East and North Africa, especially Saudi Arabia, Kuwait, Iraq and Algeria, undertaking the work in the early months of 1975, a few months after the end of the 1973–4 price hike, and publishing its findings in August 1975. Its analysis embraced such issues as the deliberate sabotaging of oilfields as well as the risk of Soviet intervention and its conclusions were robust: 'Military operations to rescue the United States (much less its key allies) from an airtight oil embargo would combine high costs with high risks. US strategic reserves would be stripped. Prospects would be poor, and plights of far-reaching political, economic, social, psychological, and perhaps military conse-quences the penalty for failure.'[3]

Such an analysis permeated US thinking on security but any comprehensive response was hindered by inter-service differences. The US Navy and Marine Corps saw their roles as having expeditionary potential and the US Army was primarily involved in planning for a war with the Soviet Union in Western and Central Europe and had little integrated air transport capability. The US Air Force had a concern with long-range strike but its logistics capabilities were far more directed at supporting its own forces overseas rather than making a priority of the rapid movement of army personnel.

Even so, the need for oil security was such that President Carter issued Presidential Directive 18 in 1977 which required the armed forces to engage in systematic planning and organizing directed towards operations in areas beyond the main spheres of US military operations, the implied emphasis being on the Persian Gulf region. Even though the United States still regarded the Shah's Iran as being a substantial bulwark against either regional instability or Soviet interference, the experience of the early 1970s demonstrated that this was not sufficient for US security needs.

Following a period of planning and argument, the Joint Chiefs of Staff agreed to a Joint Rapid Deployment Task Force (JRDTF), more popularly known as the Rapid Deployment Force, which was assembled by pooling forces from all four branches of the military. While this would be based in the United States, there would be extensive planning for overseas actions, a degree of pre-placement of stores and equipment in locations such as Diego Garcia in the Indian Ocean and a capability to airlift troops at very short notice, followed by a rapid sealift capacity. The JRDTF was established right at the end of the Carter presidency but had little impact on the cluster of crises at that time, especially the Iranian Revolution, the Soviet occupation of Afghanistan and the further substantial increase in oil prices of 1979–80.

These price rises were a consequence not of OPEC political action but of shortages arising from a combination of the disruption during the Iranian Revolution and the onset of the bitter eight-year Iran–Iraq War, a period of upheaval that was accompanied in the United States by the election of Ronald Reagan. While the Reagan administration came to power partly on a platform of increased defence spending and of facing down the Soviet Union, the impact of the Iranian Revolution and the parallel increases in oil prices meant that the administration had a particular concern with oil security. Indeed, the first Military Posture Statement of the US Joint Chiefs of Staff in the Reagan era, the Statement for Fiscal Year 1982 (published in February 1981) placed a remarkable emphasis on resource security. This pointed to the sustainability of the Soviet resource base in contrast to the increasing US dependence on imports, with the overall emphasis on energy resources, especially oil.[4]

The concern with the US resource base, when compared with the Soviet Union, went well beyond oil and placed emphasis on the potential for Soviet destabilization of supply centres for US resources. In addition to being self-sufficient in fuel minerals (oil, gas and coal), the Soviet Union was virtually self-sufficient in almost all the other minerals required for its industrial base, needing to import only six minerals that were defence-related:

> In contrast, the United States relies on foreign sources to supply in excess of 50 percent of its needs for some 32 minerals essential for our military and industrial base. Particularly important mineral imports (for example, diamonds, cobalt, platinum, chromium and manganese) come from southern Africa, where the Soviet Union and its surrogates have established substantial influence, and where US access, given the inherent instabilities within the region, is by no means assured.[5]

The phraseology of most of the Military Posture Statement was for the most part directed at the threat from the Soviet

Union, and although much of it covered the range of resources required by the United States, there was an underlying emphasis on the Persian Gulf and its oil resources. This was at a time of conspicuous dismay and a degree of impotence in Washington over events in Iran. The fall of the Shah was rapid, unexpected and total. Moreover, it was made worse by the hostage crisis and the costly failure of the attempt to rescue the detained diplomats in Operation Eagle Claw in April 1980. The United States no longer had a close ally in the region in the form of the Shah's Iran, and there was a powerful argument that the Rapid Deployment Force was simply not sufficient to ensure the security of the Persian Gulf region. The Reagan administration therefore opted to elevate the force into an entirely new unified military command, Central Command (CENTCOM), which would maintain US security interests across the whole of the Middle East. Indeed, CENTCOM was responsible for US interests in an arc of 19 countries from Kenya in the south-west right through to Pakistan in the east.

By the end of 1984, CENTCOM could already call on four army divisions and a brigade, and a marine corps division and brigade, together with substantial air and sea support. Rapid deployment was retained, especially with high levels of alert maintained within the Army's 82nd Airborne Division. At any one time, a complete army brigade of around 4,000 troops was on standby, with air-mobile artillery, air defences and the necessary airlift available for movement at 20 hours' notice.

By the end of the decade, shortly before the crisis with Iraq, CENTCOM had been further expanded to include three carrier battle groups, the Third Army, the Ninth Air Force, a Marine Amphibious Force and many reconnaissance, Special Forces and intelligence units. Combined with extensive logistic pre-positioning, including the establishment of a permanent Maritime Pre-positioning Force of 13 ships of up to 46,000 tons laden weight, CENTCOM was considered to be in a position to secure US interests in the Persian Gulf region, either in the face of Soviet aggression or in the event of regional crises. Although the great majority of the forces allocated to CENTCOM were normally stationed in the continental United States, and the CENTCOM headquarters was in Florida, the end result was a capability centred on the security of Persian Gulf oil, a capability that outlasted the Soviet Union and was available for the 1991 Gulf War and the war on terror more than a decade later.

Perhaps the most important state in the region, at least in terms of oil wealth, was Saudi Arabia, but sensitivities about the basing of foreign troops on Saudi soil were already evident well before the advent of the al-Qaida movement. As a result, there was detailed cooperation with Saudi forces in terms of equipment and training, and construction programmes were organized that provided facilities that were far larger than those required by the Saudis themselves. Given the provision of such facilities, it was not necessary to run the risk of basing US forces in the Kingdom; instead, they could be moved in at a time of crisis, as was the case in the closing months of 1990 after the Iraqi occupation of Kuwait. Without the years of preparation, the movement of coalition forces into Saudi Arabia and the subsequent eviction of Iraqi forces from Kuwait would have been a much longer, more difficult and costly project.

The Persian Gulf after the 1991 war

The US-coalition success of the Gulf War in 1991 appeared to vindicate the perceived US need to ensure the security of the Persian Gulf, even though the Cold War was now over. Given the success in defeating the Iraqi armed forces and the absence of the Soviet threat, the United States might have been expected to maintain a somewhat lower key concern with the

Persian Gulf, but this was not the case for four broad reasons. First, the actual experience of the 1991 war, as discussed in the last chapter, was salutary for the US military, both in terms of the political and psychological impact of the Scud missiles and the potential for Iraqi use of chemical and biological weapons if the coalition had moved beyond expelling the forces from Kuwait to threaten regime survival.

Secondly, the regime itself survived more or less intact and had sufficient military capabilities to suppress the post-war Kurdish and Shi'a rebellions. This caused some surprise in US and Western European military circles and stems from a failure to grasp the Iraqi war aims at the actual time of the outbreak of the war in January 1991. While the original invasion and occupation of Kuwait was expected to consolidate an enlarged Iraq with formidable oil reserves – around one fifth of total world oil reserves at that time – once the substantial coalition force was deployed to the region, the Iraqi war aim became one of regime survival rather than the permanent integration of Kuwait into an enlarged Iraq. As a result, the main Iraqi forces deployed in and around Kuwait were largely conscript forces, whereas the eight much better equipped Republican Guard divisions played a much smaller role. Some were involved in the final days of the war and took serious casualties, but most of the soldiers in these eight divisions survived. Moreover, a range of elite units, including brigades attached to security and intelligence services, played little or no part in the entire war. In effect, weak forces were sacrificed to ensure regime survival. That more limited war aim was achieved.

The United States and its coalition partners therefore faced an Iraq which may have been economically weakened but was implacably opposed to western strategic interests. This was an extraordinary change from just three years previously, when Iraq was closely allied to France and the United States and was getting a wide range of equipment and intelligence support in its war with the much greater regional threat to US interests at that time – Iran.

The third factor was precisely that the 1991 Gulf War had certainly weakened Iraq, but had actually left Iran in a stronger position. It was not that Iran was in any way an immediate threat to US interests. The costs of the 1980–8 Iran–Iraq War had been terrible, particularly in terms of the several hundred thousand young men who had died in the bitter trench warfare of the early 1980s. Nevertheless, revolutionary Iran was seen as a potentially antagonistic state that was certainly in a stronger position as a result of the 1991 war.

Finally, there was the matter of the global trends in oil exploration, reserves and production, this being an issue that was not just relevant in the early 1990s but has grown considerably since and now underlies so much of US policy in the region.

Security of supply and the China factor

Establishing the size of world oil reserves is subject to discussion, disagreement and controversy, and any statistics that provide estimates over a number of years are apt to show major changes. Table 3.1 gives estimates from one of the most widely used sources, the annual *British Petroleum Statistical Review of World Energy*, for the fifteen leading holders of oil reserves in 2005, with figures for the same countries a decade and two decades earlier. Changes include the substantial upwards estimates of reserves for some Middle East countries and Venezuela, quite marked upwards estimates for Libya and Nigeria, and a marked decline for Mexico.

Some explanation for the increases lies in the substantial exploration activity that followed the price rises of the 1970s and early 1980s, and Mexico's decline was partially due to new estimates of the difficulty of recovering some reserves. At the

Table 3.1 World oil reserves (billion barrels)			
	1985	1995	2005
Saudi Arabia	171.5	261.5	264.2
Iran	59.0	93.7	137.5
Iraq	65.0	100.0	115.0
Kuwait	92.5	96.5	101.5
United Arab Emirates	33.0	98.1	97.8
Venezuela	55.4	66.3	79.7
Russia	n/a	n/a	74.7
Kazakhstan	n/a	n/a	39.6
Libya	21.3	29.5	39.1
Nigeria	16.6	20.8	39.1
United States	36.4	29.8	29.3
Canada	9.6	10.5	16.5
China	17.1	16.3	16.0
Qatar	4.5	3.7	15.2
Mexico	55.6	48.8	13.7

Source: BP Statistical Review of World Energy, June 2006

same time, there were suspicions that changes in the Iraqi, UAE and Iranian reserves may have had much to do with internal OPEC politics, although the higher figures are widely accepted across most of the world oil industry. It is also worth noting that some recent estimates hugely increase Canadian and Venezuelan reserves, these relating to Canadian tar sand and Venezuelan Orinoco heavy oil deposits. It is not uniformly accepted that such low quality reserves are comparable to more conventional deposits.

Finally, there is a strong and vocal school of thought that is suspicious of most of the higher sets of reserves, with an added view that we are already close to, or even at, what is termed 'peak oil' – that time in oil exploration and production when reserves are at their peak and will decline quite rapidly from then on. The point about peak oil is that it implies an increasing risk of scarcity and therefore substantial price rises.

Whatever the variations in analysis, it is clear that the Persian Gulf region has a remarkable abundance of oil, over 60 per cent of proved reserves on BP's estimates, and if Russia, Kazakhstan and Venezuela are included, a cluster of just eight countries – Saudi Arabia, Iran, Iraq, Kuwait, the Emirates, Venezuela, Russia and Kazakhstan – have around 80 per cent of world oil reserves. By comparison the United States has under 3 per cent of world reserves but is pumping 8.0 per cent of world annual production and China, with less than 2 per cent, accounts for 4.6 per cent of world annual production. In short, neither the United States nor China are giants in terms of reserves, but are significant producers from a relatively small reserve base and are therefore rapidly depleting those reserves.

Moreover, the real issue here concerns trends over years and decades. For the United States, the increase in import dependency began to be a serious issue in the early 1970s and has become much more significant in the past decade. In 2000, the United States imported around 58 per cent of its oil requirements, and this is expected to grow to about 74 per cent by 2020. While much of the imported oil comes from Venezuela and West Africa, the Persian Gulf is increasing in importance.

For China, the move towards import dependency has been very much more rapid, partly because of smaller domestic reserves but mainly because of the rapid pace of economic growth and the parallel increase in demand for oil. China was self-sufficient in oil until 1993 but will need to import half of all its requirements by 2010. Moreover, China may have made extensive overtures to Venezuela, Sudan and other non-Gulf producers, but its major relationship has been with Iran and its overall dependency on Persian Gulf oil is expected to grow.

From a US perspective, a much broader issue is relevant – the increasing dependency of all the major industrialized and industrializing states, except Russia, on Persian Gulf oil. With the decline in North Sea oil reserves, Western Europe is even more dependent on imported oil than two decades ago; Japan, South Korea, Taiwan and the growing economies of countries such as the Philippines, Vietnam and Thailand all need increasing imports of oil; and India's needs are expanding rapidly. In other words, much of the world's economic growth is predicated on oil supplies from the Middle East and Africa. Africa's significance may be increasing, as is indicated not least by the US decision to establish a new unified military command for the continent, with interesting echoes of the setting up of CENTCOM more than twenty years ago. Even so, the total reserves of sub-Saharan Africa are small compared with the Persian Gulf region, and that is the region that will supply most of the world's oil for as long as the current addiction continues.

Russia may eventually have the capacity to play a more major role in international relations, and countries such as India and Brazil are becoming steadily more significant, but the one state that may eventually match the United States is China, and the primary Chinese vulnerability in terms of political economy is its external energy dependency. From Beijing's perspective, the Gulf is also crucial, whatever efforts go into securing African oil supplies. While China does not have the military capacity to exert any serious degree of influence in the Persian Gulf, it does have considerable economic power and has been notably successful at concluding long-term economic agreements over oil and gas supplies, especially with Iran.

Conclusion

From a US perspective, whether of the neoconservative or assertive-realist variety, its long-term relationship with China, its more general influence on the world economy and its own energy security all relate strongly to retaining security dominance in the Persian Gulf. This has been evident since the mid-1970s, with an interest going back a further thirty years, and is reflected in the establishment of the Rapid Deployment Force, its development into Central Command, and the bringing together of a massive coalition in response to the Iraqi takeover of Kuwait in 1990 and to the 9/11 attacks. Indeed, it can be argued that the nature of that response and its consequences cannot be properly understood without recognizing the singular importance of the Persian Gulf region.

PART II
Events

CHAPTER FOUR

From Kabul to Baghdad

Introduction

Part I examined the background to the 9/11 attacks in terms of the US political context, the capabilities of the US military including the transition from the Cold War to the post-Cold War world and the specific concern with the security of the Persian Gulf in relation to international oil security. Concerning US politics, three elements were considered relevant. One was the continuing element of assertive realism applied to perceptions of US security, in that the United States under President Clinton saw itself as the world's sole superpower. Its military experience in Somalia in 1993 had been salutary and there was a marked perception of the need to act primarily in its own interests, even if there was still a widespread multilateral engagement on numerous issues.

The second was the rise in influence of a strong neoconservative thread, principally through a series of interest groups and think tanks. From this perspective there was every prospect of a New American Century with the United States providing historic global leadership that would essentially reshape much of the world in a liberal market American mould. Finally, there was a strong view among neoconservatives and others that the 1991 war with Iraq was unfinished business and that there was a requirement to act against the Saddam Hussein regime.

The military transformation after the ending of the Cold War involved moves towards global power projection that might be fewer than those deployed in the Cold War years but in the face of much diminished, if somewhat uncertain, threats. Furthermore, the United States ended the twentieth century as an unrivalled military power. In doing so, however, one particular commitment was to the security of the Persian Gulf, the 1991 war with Iraq having been in some respects a damaging experience.

In overall terms, though, eight months into the Bush administration the perception in Washington was of American power that was unassailable. There was every prospect, at least from a neoconservative perspective, that the benevolent hegemon could indeed shape the world in a mission to civilize that was almost religious in its intensity. The United States, that 'City on the Hill', could do God's work in the world. Others could be prey to history – the United States could make history. Then came 9/11.

9/11 and its impact

When the first of the hijacked aircraft crashed into the North Tower of the World Trade Center in New York, it was seen initially as a terrible accident. Within minutes, the burning building was being screened live on television, but there was also an immediate recall of a previous incident when a B-25 bomber had crashed into the Empire State Building in July 1945 in fog, killing 13 people. Shortly after the North Tower was hit, a second plane crashed into the South Tower and the immediate response was that this was some kind of attack. By the time the South Tower was hit, the unfolding events were being seen live on television across the United States and around the world.

Timing was significant in that it was around 9 am in New York, 8 am in Chicago and the Mid-West, 7 am Mountain Time and 6 am Pacific Time. By the time the more seriously damaged South Tower collapsed, the recognition of the scale of the attack was becoming clear, especially as news spread of the plane hitting the Pentagon. Finally, the North Tower collapsed, with people across the country knowing that many thousands had died. The attacks were both devastating and unexpected, and their impact has been compared to the only other instance affecting the United States in modern times – the Japanese attack on Pearl Harbor that resulted in the Pacific War.

In fact, Pearl Harbor is a poor comparison – the 9/11 atrocity had a much greater impact at a visceral level for several reasons. One, obviously, is that it was witnessed live on television, but there were others. The Pearl Harbor assault was launched by another state that was already in serious political confrontation with the United States. While the attack itself may have been an extraordinary surprise, there were already tensions between the United States and Japan, the war in Europe was two years old and Japan itself had been at war in China for four years. Furthermore, Pearl Harbor was a conventional military operation against a military base.

The 9/11 attacks also included an assault on the Pentagon, and this certainly had a much greater effect on the US military than most analysts have acknowledged. It was an indication of unexpected vulnerability that the centre of worldwide US military power could be hit by a small group of determined paramilitaries armed only with parcel knives. For the American public, though, the World Trade Center was far more fundamental to its own perception of US vulnerability. The twin towers had almost entirely replaced the old Empire State Building as the symbol of US international business leadership. Furthermore, just one part of the Pentagon was damaged whereas the World Trade Center was completely destroyed. In terms of its impact on US culture, 9/11 had a far greater impact than Pearl Harbor, even if that had been a rude and final awakening from nearly two decades of isolationism.

Moreover, for those of a neoconservative persuasion who were looking forward to the welcome and even unstoppable evolution of the New American Century, 9/11 was almost unbelievable. Just a few months into the Bush administration, as everything seemed to be going so well, the United States had suffered an appalling attack. It was also an attack that was deeply felt by countries closest to it, especially in Europe where the French response was to be encapsulated in the *Le Monde* headline, 'We are all Americans now.'

In view of all of these circumstances, the response from the United States was likely to be forthright in the extreme, but it is also relevant to examine the 9/11 attacks not from a US perspective but from that of the al-Qaida movement. What, in essence, were the planners in that movement hoping to achieve, and was a robust response from the United States an action that was anticipated and possibly even welcomed?

Al-Qaida motives for 9/11

The extent to which the 9/11 operation was organized from an al-Qaida movement that was then centred on camps in Afghanistan is debatable. While there were clearly many connections, the planning and implementation of the attack was essentially a matter for a group that was at least semi-independent of any central al-Qaida organization. Osama bin Laden's first public statement after the 9/11 attacks came on 24 September and was mainly directed at events in Pakistan. Following 9/11, the Pakistani military ruler, General Pervez Musharraf, had declared support for the United States in its war on terror and this declaration resulted in riots that were violently suppressed. Bin Laden's statement referred to those killed, making specific mention of the term 'crusader' that had been used by President Bush in announcing the start of the war on terror: 'We urge these brothers to be considered the first martyrs in the battle of Islam against the neo-Crusader Jewish campaign led by Bush, the biggest Crusader, under the banner of the cross. This battle can be seen as merely one of the battles of eternal Islam.'[1]

A further bin Laden statement on 7 October praised the 9/11 attacks without taking responsibility for them, a stance similar to those at the time of the Khobar Towers and Nairobi/Dar es Salaam bombings.[2]

In not seeking to represent the 9/11 attacks as centrally organized, bin Laden could imply that the al-Qaida movement was much broader than those groups centred on Afghanistan and that these were part of a loose and broadly based movement that permeated much of the global Islamic community. At the same time, it was inevitable that the attacks would have a profound effect on the United States, with two possible implications for the al-Qaida movement.

One was that it was a powerful indication of the capacity of the movement to attack the far enemy, hitting its military headquarters and its most important financial centre. For those many supporters of the movement and its affiliates, this was a remarkable demonstration of power, and many of bin Laden's subsequent statements made reference to the retribution wrought by the attacks. This was retribution not just for immediate offences against Islam but went much further. In his 7 October statement, for example, bin Laden said: 'What America is tasting today is but a fraction of what we have tasted for decades. For over eighty years our *Umma* has endured this humiliation and contempt. Its sons have been killed, its blood has been shed, its holy sanctuaries have been violated, all in a manner contrary to that revealed by God, without anyone listening.'[3]

By striking at the heart of the United States, the 9/11 attackers had demonstrated in an extraordinary way the ability of the movement to respond to those decades of humiliation.

Moreover, this was the world's only superpower, the former power of the Soviet Union having been crippled by the war in Afghanistan fifteen years earlier.

This relates directly to the second implication of the 9/11 attacks for al-Qaida, the confident expectation that the United States would react with extraordinary force to this assault on its best-known international business centre, its military head-quarters and its prestige. For al-Qaida and the wider jihadist movement, the impact of the war in Afghanistan in the 1980s was immensely relevant. Over the best part of a decade, resist-ance fighters had opposed a large army of Soviet troops, mostly conscripts, and had eventually forced their retreat. This might not have been possible without the consistent aid from the United States, aid which had even included a direct connection between the CIA and bin Laden. Neither would it have been possible without the staunch support of Pakistan, especially the work of the Inter-Services Intelligence organization (ISI).[4] For Pakistan, this earlier war in Afghanistan was a strategic asset as it worked closely with the United States and increased its influence in Afghanistan as the Soviet occupation faltered. Working with the United States and ultimately helping defeat the Soviet Union was greatly beneficial in longer-term compe-tition with neighbouring India.

For bin Laden and al-Qaida in 2001, though, the main mes-sage from the conflict in the 1980s was that the Soviet Union had been crippled by a successful guerrilla war and this had been the deciding factor in its ultimate collapse. Other analysts might point out that collapse may certainly have been aided by the Afghan failure but this was far from the only factor. From an al-Qaida perspective, though, other causes were ignored and the Afghan War was seen as the first great victory in a struggle against foreign occupiers and other threats to Islam that was still in its early years and might well last a century. Put simply, a superpower had invaded one of the lands of Islam and had been repulsed. Now, the surviving superpower, which had military forces occupying Saudi Arabia, had experienced a grievous assault and would, no doubt, retaliate against the al-Qaida movement and its hosts, the Taliban regime in Afghanistan.

That, in turn, would require an occupation by US forces which would, in all probability, lead to a rerun of the 1980s. While the power of the United States military might be much more substantial than the poorly trained conscript armies of the old Soviet Union, a guerrilla war would still ensue and over some years the United States would be defeated, crippling not just its influence in South-West and Central Asia but perhaps even leading to its demise as a superpower. In essence, 9/11 would result in the 'far enemy' coming to Afghanistan. There would be little further need to attack the United States, even though the symbolism of the 9/11 attacks would empower supporters across the Islamic world. Instead, the United States would come to al-Qaida.

Regime termination in Afghanistan

If this was a serious calculation on the part of commanding elements of the al-Qaida movement, then it involved a critical yet natural mistake. Intellectuals within the movement would have recognized the nature of the Bush administration, with its forceful embracing of the idea of a New American Century, and would have been confident in a vigorous and robust military response. Moreover, they would have looked back to the Iraqi occupation of Kuwait and the extraordinary response from the United States and its western coalition partners. True, that coalition had included states such as Syria and Egypt, but the core of the response was the assembling of over half a million troops, well over a thousand aircraft and a hundred warships. If that was the American-led response to a distant invasion, albeit one with important implications for oil security, then a hugely significant attack on the United States itself would, on this line of thinking, involve a response of a similar order. This time, though, the aim would be the termination of the Taliban regime and the destruction of the core of the al-Qaida movement, not the removal of Iraqi forces and a subsequent withdrawal, a military operation which in 1991 had stopped well short of regime termination.

It is possible that the Bush administration and the US military planners might have responded with an operation on a scale not greatly less than that in 1991, but there were many factors that would make this hugely difficult. The facilities available in Saudi Arabia in late 1990 were enormous, partly as a result of the detailed CENTCOM planning of the 1980s (see chapter 3). The United States had a huge range of sealift and airlift capabilities, it was aided by many other states and it would be fighting a conventional war against a state equipped with largely obsolete equipment and, for the most part, poorly trained troops that would be fighting in an environment that lent itself to the abilities of the US forces that had prepared for war against a much more powerful state, the Soviet Union, over the previous forty years.

Afghanistan, on the other hand, was a mountainous country with poor communications and no direct access to the sea. To the west was Iran that was hardly likely to cooperate, and to the north were Central Asian states that were uncertain in their support. The main route to Afghanistan was through Pakistan, but bringing several combat divisions through that country from the distant ports would be a logistic feat that would take many months. Even with all the facilities in Saudi Arabia and the CENTCOM pre-planning, the US-led coalition had taken five months to prepare for the 1991 war. Ten years later, the 9/11 attacks came barely two months before the start of winter, when many of the routes into Afghanistan would be difficult if not impassable. For these many reasons, the war would be fought in a very different manner, and this might well not be conducive to the hopes and expectations of the al-Qaida leadership. The Taliban regime in Afghanistan would indeed be terminated – there was no other option given the shock in the United States and the outlook of the Bush administration – but it would follow a different route to that of the 1991 Gulf War.

The 2001 Afghan War

To the surprise of many commentators, and much of American public opinion, there was little evidence of an immediate US military response to 9/11. After the East African Embassy attacks, there had been an immediate if largely symbolic response in the form of cruise missile raids against an al-Qaida camp in Afghanistan and, strangely, a veterinary pharmaceutical plant in Sudan. For nearly four weeks after 9/11, though, there was no overt military action against the Taliban and little indication of major troop movements towards the region. Instead, the US military embarked on a plan that had four major components. The first was to begin the development of temporary bases that would overcome some of the logistic problems, with Central Asian republics such as Uzbekistan being important components. Although the initial intention was to have such bases to aid regime termination in Afghanistan, a supplementary advantage would be to build up US military and political influence in Central Asia. This was useful in the longer term as a way of counterbalancing Russian and Chinese influence, especially as the southern regions of Central Asia included parts of the oil-rich Caspian Basin.

The second component was to make available a sufficient quantity of air power to ensure that a prolonged bombing campaign in Afghanistan was possible. Part of that was achieved by deploying aircraft carrier battle groups, part came from added deployments to bases within reach of Afghanistan and part involved the availability of long-range strategic bombers operating from Britain and Diego Garcia. Thirdly, the United States was prepared to deploy ground troops in Afghanistan, but in limited numbers. Some troop movements began towards the end of September but the numbers were initially small and most of these were Special Forces assigned to aid anti-Taliban elements within Afghanistan and also to direct bombing raids onto appropriate targets.

The final element in the US war plan was the unexpected decision to support the Northern Alliance with a very substantial programme of rearmament and other forms of logistic support, right down even to providing new uniforms. By the time of the 9/11 attacks, the bitter Afghan civil war had been under way between the Taliban and the Northern Alliance since the mid-1990s, but the Northern Alliance was increasingly restricted in its areas of operations and was clearly losing the conflict. The addition of copious US support made a fundamental difference to the civil war, with much of the armaments and equipment being provided from Russia if primarily financed by the United States.

Within four weeks of the onset of the war on 7 October 2001, the Northern Alliance was making substantial gains and was starting to encroach on territory that had been in Taliban hands for several years. The Northern Alliance advances were hugely aided by US air raids that involved precision bombing of individual Taliban assets, such as arms dumps and vehicle concentrations as well as bridges, and large-scale air strikes on Taliban militia concentrations using carpet bombing, cluster bombs and other area-impact munitions. The intensity of the precision US air attacks was such that supplies of key precision-guided munitions were run down very quickly, so much so that stocks held in reserve in Kuwait had to be used within a few weeks of the start of the war.

Although rapid progress was being made from a US standpoint, opposition to the war was already developing in the region, with governments in Pakistan and Jordan responding by detaining some of the more militant local leaders. Such opposition was aided by the regular reporting of civilian casualties on Middle East satellite TV news channels such as Al-Jazeera – even in the first two weeks of the war there were reported to be six examples of mis-targeting, including UN and Red Cross facilities. It was also evident that US attacks included targets that were of economic significance, such as a hydroelectric power station near Kandahar.

Until around 8 November, there were indications of Taliban retreats but these did not amount to wholesale gains for the Northern Alliance and other anti-Taliban groups. This changed radically in the five-day period from 8 to 13 November when most Taliban militia withdrew from the non-Pashtun areas of Afghanistan, sometimes in the wake of major conflicts in the north of the country.[5] For the most part, though, Taliban elements simply melted away, most famously in the case of the capital city of Kabul, where the militias evacuated the city in a single night, and subsequently dispersed with their light arms intact, very few of them being engaged in conflict with US or local forces.

By the latter part of November, some seven weeks after the start of the war and ten weeks after the 9/11 attacks, the view from Washington was that regime termination in Afghanistan was virtually complete, even if some towns and cities were still under a degree of Taliban control. There was a further anticipation that the substantive destruction of the al-Qaida movement in Afghanistan was only a matter of time, with Osama bin Laden and the Taliban leader, Mullah Omar, likely to be killed or detained in the near future. The military achievements in Afghanistan in the middle two weeks of November were regarded as little short of spectacular. They were a cause

of substantial celebration in the United States, although this
was marred by the impact of a series of letters containing
anthrax that infected a number of people in the United States,
mainly workers for the US Mail.

Even so, the overt successes in Afghanistan meant that
many opinion-formers were already pointing to the need to
extend the war on terror to Iraq. This was a natural extension
of the views that had developed, especially in neoconservative
circles, in the late 1990s, but this was now boosted by the
progress in Afghanistan. At the same time, the very rise of this
viewpoint within the Bush administration was sufficient to
cause concern in some European capitals, especially Paris and
Berlin, where the heartfelt support for the United States that
was in evidence in the immediate wake of the 9/11 atrocities
was beginning to ebb.

In Afghanistan itself, US Special Forces were used in many
parts of the country, working with Northern Alliance forces
and other groups opposed to the Taliban. On 25 November, a
substantial force of regular ground troops – in this case from
the US Marine Corps – took control of Kandahar Airport, with
other troops drawn from the Marine Corps and the US Army
deploying to key towns and cities including Kabul in the following month. At the same time, a bitter conflict was taking
place between anti-Taliban militias, aided by US forces, and
Taliban and al-Qaida militias in the White Mountains area of
south-east Afghanistan around Tora Bora. Much of the early
part of December was taken up with fighting between the
opposing forces, with US bombing raids being used to kill
Taliban and al-Qaida supporters, but with a number of anti-
Taliban militia being killed in friendly-fire incidents.

At one stage, the effect of the bombing had been such that
the anti-Taliban militia were able to agree a ceasefire with their
weaker opponents but this was overruled by US military commanders who elected to continue with the bombing campaign

while bringing in larger numbers of American and British troops. Earlier in the war, the US Air Force had used area bombing on many targets and had also, on three occasions, used the BLU-82 slurry bomb, at the time the most destructive conventional weapon in use anywhere in the world. The BLU-82 was used seven more times in rapid succession around Tora Bora, combined with extensive area bombing. What was apparent was that the US military approach had two specific components – avoiding the surrender of al-Qaida units and substantial recourse to heavy aerial bombardment.

In spite of this overwhelming air power, early reports suggested that as many as 1,500 of the militias fighting at Tora Bora had escaped, many of them into the frontier districts of western Pakistan, with perhaps 200 killed. In more general terms, analysts pointed to a Taliban death toll throughout eleven weeks of war of around 5,000 as well as several hundred al-Qaida militia. Some thousands of Taliban militia were in custody but, given that the Taliban could previously have called on at least 50,000 armed supporters, it was clear that the great majority had gone to ground.

Peace at last?

By the end of 2001, there were three somewhat contrasting views as to likely developments in Afghanistan. For the Bush administration, the Taliban regime had been terminated, the country had been liberated and the al-Qaida movement had suffered a massive blow, even if the most senior leadership, including Osama bin Laden, remained at liberty. The first three months of the declared war on terror had been remarkably successful and the main lines of arguments concerned how and where to extend that war.

The second view was more common among experienced UN officials and others with a thorough knowledge of the region, and among Afghan officials, including those returning to the country from exile. This view was that there was a critical danger of a political and security vacuum developing if Afghanistan did not get very substantial aid as well as a large stabilization force that could help bring a sufficient degree of order to the country to allow reconstruction and development to proceed. Such a force would need 30,000 or more troops in a peacekeeping and stabilization role, and needed to be in place in a matter of months. What was planned in December 2001 was far smaller than that – perhaps 5,000 troops centred primarily on Kabul.

From this perspective there was a recognition of the huge costs of more than two decades of war, with an added concern that the flooding of armaments into the country in the last three months of 2001 would make stability even more difficult to achieve. Regional specialists also recognized that the conduct of the war was having an impact that went well beyond Afghanistan. There were reasonably reputable estimates that at least 3,000 civilians had been killed in the war, principally through aerial bombing, and it was becoming apparent that many thousands were being imprisoned without prisoner-of-war status, with hundreds being transported to the US base at Guantanamo Bay in Cuba where they were beyond the influence of the US civil judiciary.

Finally, some security analysts were pointing to the remarkable manner in which the Taliban militias had withdrawn from the conflict. Wherever Taliban elements had faced a potentially overwhelming combination of US air power and Northern Alliance forces, they had simply chosen not to fight. What was surprising was the manner in which they could withdraw into local communities, sometimes across the border in Pakistan but most commonly in Afghanistan itself. Moreover, as the Northern Alliance and US forces moved across those parts of Afghanistan where the al-Qaida movement had had its training camps, they almost invariably found the bases deserted. Not only had the Taliban dispersed, but so had the al-Qaida movement. What was perhaps not fully realized at the time was that, prior to 9/11, the al-Qaida movement was maintaining camps in Afghanistan mainly to train paramilitaries from abroad to aid the Taliban in the closing stages of the Afghan Civil War rather than for a more global jihad. That might come in due course, but the short-term aim had been to ensure the integrity of Afghanistan, with the external forces also available to counter a major US military presence. It is probable that if there had been such a presence, the al-Qaida strategists would have expected a sustained growth in paramilitary recruits from across western Asia and the Middle East and North Africa, with a guerrilla campaign developing over several years.

What was clear by the end of 2001 was that the Taliban had largely melted away without suffering a conventional military defeat and consequent surrender and most of the al-Qaida elements had simply disappeared. While thousands of Taliban and al-Qaida supporters had been detained, and some significant elements of the al-Qaida leadership had been killed or captured, there was a strong argument already being aired that the war was not actually over, but that only its first phase was coming to an end. As one analysis concluded in late December 2001:

> there is a degree of stability in Kabul and some of the larger towns, but this has been accompanied by a rapid revival of warlordism and banditry in much of the country. The small UN-backed stabilisation force now being assembled in Kabul may eventually extend its work to a few other centres of population, but it would require many tens of thousands of troops to bring order to the country as a whole. There is no international commitment to such a programme.[6]

There was certainly no recognition in Washington of the need for a large stabilization force: 'this would be unacceptable to the Pentagon, which is concerned primarily to continue the search for the Taliban and al-Qaida leadership, insofar as it is still in Afghanistan. This determination even extends to having ensured that the international force, ostensibly led by the UK, is under the final command of the Pentagon.'[7]

Stabilization and post-conflict peace-building was clearly not the priority for the Bush administration, and the first six months of 2002 were to be a key period in determining how the administration's declared war on terror would develop over the following two years. Much of this would follow the 2002 State of the Union Address by President Bush to the US Congress.

The State of the Union – extending the war

The 29 January State of the Union address to both Houses of Congress was in many ways the high point of the war on terror. Delivered in the style of a victory speech and interrupted by more than 70 bursts of applause, President Bush pointed to the remarkable success in Afghanistan, both in terminating the Taliban regime and dispersing the al-Qaida movement. Most of the speech was devoted to the success of the war on terror so far, but its most important aspect was the manner in which that war, so far directed almost entirely against the Taliban and al-Qaida in Afghanistan, was to be extended to a global campaign embracing many terror organizations and even a number of states: 'Our nation will continue to be steadfast and patient and persistent in the pursuit of two great objectives. First, we will shut down terrorist camps, disrupt terrorist plans, and bring terrorists to justice. And, second, we must prevent the terrorists and regimes who seek chemical, biological or nuclear weapons from threatening the United States and the world.'[8] President Bush was quick to point to the extensive range of terror organizations and countries in which they operated:

'Our military has put the terror training camps of Afghanistan out of business, yet camps still exist in at least a dozen countries. A terrorist underworld – including groups like Hamas, Hezbollah, Islamic Jihad, Jaish-u-Mohammed – operates in remote jungles and deserts, and hides in the centers of large cities.'[9]

He cited a range of military actions already being taken, including US troops training Philippine Army troops in counter-terrorism, assisting the Bosnian government in seizing terrorists planning to attack the US embassy in Bosnia, and using US Navy ships to block arms shipments to Somalia to prevent the establishment of training camps there. While he called for united support in pursuit of this war, he made it abundantly clear that the United States reserved the right to take action when it saw fit:

> My hope is that all nations will heed our call, and eliminate the terrorist parasites who threaten their countries and our own. Many nations are acting forcefully. Pakistan is now cracking down on terror, and I admire the strong leadership of President Musharraf.
>
> But some governments will be timid in the face of terror. And make no mistake about it: If they do not act, we will.[10]

Much of the rhetoric was to be expected, given the extent of the 9/11 atrocities and the nature of the Bush administration, but what surprised many governments and opinion-formers outside the United States was the manner in which the war on terror was to be extended to include unacceptable regimes. Three were singled out for specific mention – North Korea, Iran and especially Iraq:

> States like these, and their terrorist allies, constitute an axis of evil, arming to threaten the peace of the world. By seeking weapons of mass destruction, these regimes pose a grave and growing danger. They could provide these arms to terrorists, giving them the means to match their hatred. They could

attack our allies or attempt to blackmail the United States. In any of these cases, the price of indifference would be cata-strophic.[11]

While advocating cooperation to limit the risk of proliferation, President Bush emphasized the likely need for action: We'll be deliberate, yet time is not on our side. I will not wait on events, while dangers gather. I will not stand by, as perils draw closer and closer. The United States of America will not permit the world's most dangerous regimes to threaten us with the world's most destructive weapons.[12]

Elsewhere in the speech he announced the largest increase in the defence budget in two decades and the near doubling of the budget for homeland security, pointing to the attempt to destroy an airliner bound for the United States just over a month earlier as an indicator of the need for new vigilance.

While the 2002 State of the Union address undoubtedly served a very important function of reassuring the domestic audience, following the visceral impact of the 9/11 attacks, it brought a sense of unease to many outside the United States, an unease that was further fostered by President Bush's address at the West Point Military Academy four months later. On that occasion, Bush pointed to the probable incidence of terrorist cells in 60 or more countries, and claimed that the United States faced a threat without precedent, given the asymmetric nature of the new challenge:

> Enemies in the past needed great armies and great industrial capabilities to endanger the American people and our nation. The attacks of September the 11th required a few hundred thousand dollars in the hands of a few dozen evil and deluded men. All of the chaos and suffering they caused came at much less than the cost of a single tank. The dangers have not passed. This government and the American people are on watch, we are ready, because we know the terrorists have more money and more men and more plans.[13]

Moreover, while defensive measures such as homeland security and missile defence would be part of the process, 'the war on terror will not be won on the defensive. We must take the battle to the enemy, disrupt his plans, and confront the worst threats before they emerge. In the world we have entered, the only path to safety is the path of action. And this nation will act.'[14] In case there was any doubt that US pre-emptive action would apply to states as well as terrorist groups, he stated forcefully that: 'All nations that decide for aggression and terror will pay a price. We will not leave the safety of America and the peace of the planet at the mercy of a few mad terrorists and tyrants. We will lift this dark threat from our country and from the world.'[15]

Divisions

The six-month period from January to June 2002 was a time of expansion of the war on terror and, in some senses, represented the key period in the whole of the first six years of the war when the Bush administration could consider its war going according to plan. Even so, it was also a period of emerging differences of opinion among otherwise sympathetic states, difficulties in Afghanistan, the significance of which was largely unrecognized, further activity by the supposedly dispersed and defeated al-Qaida movement and outright concern over US behaviour in many parts of the world outside America's immediate allies.

Even in mid-December 2002, there had been expressions of concern in unexpected quarters, a notable example being an unusually candid speech by the head of the British armed forces, Chief of Defence Staff Admiral Sir Michael Boyce. Speaking at the Royal United Services Institute in London, he warned of the dangers of the idea that a war on terror could be won by intensive military action while not recognizing the basic causes of the problem. He further warned that excessive force could even tend to radicalize Islamic opinion. In the wake of the State of the Union address, this view became much more widely shared across Europe and beyond. In what might be called the 'majority world' of the southern countries, many analysts and politicians saw the war on terror as more a means of increasing influence across the world, not least in Central Asia where a network of new bases was being established.

In a remarkably prescient comment that had been made very soon after the 9/11 attacks, Walden Bello had condemned the attacks as horrific, despicable and unpardonable, but had cautioned against an automatic 'iron fist' that ignored the underlying context. He pointed to the frequent use of what was seen as indiscriminate force by the United States, not least in Korea and Vietnam, and to the bitter mood throughout the Middle East and South-West Asia that pre-dated 9/11, directed partly at the United States because of its perceived dominance of the region but also against autocratic states depending on continuing US support. The analysis concluded:

> The only response that will readily contribute to global security and peace is for Washington to address not the symptoms but the roots of terrorism. It is for the United States to re-examine and substantially change its policies in the Middle East and the Third World, supporting, for a change, arrangements that will not stand in the way of the achievement of equity, justice and genuine national sovereignty for currently marginalized people. Any other way leads to endless war.[16]

While Bello was one of the most astute analysts writing from a southern perspective, especially in the immediate post-9/11 nature of his response, the State of the Union address caused more widespread concern as it appeared too much like an excuse to further the New American Century:

> Increasing numbers in the South perceive the evolving situation as no less than modern imperialism, using the full

panoply of mechanisms to bend the will and shape the global order to suit the preference and needs of the major advanced industrial nations. Moreover, this new imperialism is largely unhindered, in fact it is even aided and abetted, by the multilateral mechanisms developed over the past five decades.

Growing resentment in the South at the sense of powerlessness in the face of Northern arrogance and impunity breeds frustration, which hardly provides fertile ground for development or peace or building the international community. Now, the fear of speaking up in defence of one's own interests has been further exacerbated by the new dictum 'You are either with us or against us.'[17]

These and similar views were common across much of the south but were irrelevant if not entirely unrecognizable to the Bush administration. Moreover, the administration seemed incapable of recognizing the growing mood of anti-Americanism across much of the world. This was not just across the nations and communities beyond the cluster of countries in North America and Western Europe, since the public mood in much of Europe was also in transition. What had been substantial support for the United States in the immediate aftermath of the 9/11 attacks was rapidly evaporating as the US moved towards an apparently simplistic generalization of the need to tame the jungle by applying military force. The State of the Union and West Point addresses made it clear that pre-emptive action not just against terrorist groups but against entire states would be undertaken when the US considered it necessary.

Moreover, the conflict in Afghanistan had resulted in a substantial increase in the US presence across Central Asia, coupled with improved relations with Bulgaria and Romania in Eastern Europe. By early January 2002, over 1,000 soldiers of the US 10th Mountain Division were established at the Khanabad airbase in Uzbekistan, a new base was under construction at Bishkek in Kyrgyzstan and sites for another new base were being investigated in Tajikistan. Coupled with the establishment of bases at Bagram and Kandahar in Afghanistan, and with a US presence at several bases in Pakistan, this meant that the United States had succeeded in developing a new presence that was unexpected and pervasive across a region that was considered to be home territory both to Russia and China.

Afghanistan and al-Qaida

Meanwhile, during the course of 2002, even as the Bush administration was confident of its pursuit of the war on terror, issues in Afghanistan and the persistence of the al-Qaida movement were indicating that what had been seen as a massively successful example of regime change might be far less complete than had been assumed. An International Security Assistance Force (ISAF) was beginning to be established in Afghanistan early in 2002, but it would comprise only 5,000 troops with only five contingents above 300 in size and the rest made up of small units from a dozen other countries. By contrast, the UN Deputy Special Envoy in Afghanistan, Francesc Vendrell, was reported as saying that 30,000 would be required to give some measure of stability.

Even as this stabilization force was beginning to be established, far more US troops were engaged in continuing counter-insurgency operations against militias that had simply not gone away or been defeated. On several occasions early in 2002, the use of air strikes against presumed militia targets resulted in civilian casualties, with strong criticism coming from Hamid Karzai, the interim political leader in Kabul. Then, in early March, there was sustained fighting around Gardez involving around 1,000 US combat troops alongside about the same number of Afghan forces, together fighting a militia group apparently made up of Taliban and al-Qaida elements. The conflict was far tougher and more costly than had been anticipated, with 40 US troops killed or injured and five helicopters damaged. As the *Washington Post* reported (6 March):

> An opening advance on Saturday by Afghan and US Special Forces, intended to flush out suspected al Qaeda fighters in the town of Sirkanel, was thwarted when enemy gunfire kept coalition troops pinned down for hours. Elements of the 10th Mountain Division also were reported stopped in their tracks Saturday in a 12-hour battle outside the town of Marzak. Mortar rounds and rocket-propelled grenades landed as close as 15 yards to their position, and 13 American soldiers were injured.

The fighting around Gardez was later described as a Taliban–al-Qaida 'last stand' but it became clear in the months that followed that the conflict in Afghanistan was far from over. The problem was that this was scarcely recognized in Washington, where the focus was already on Iraq. Furthermore, there was little recognition that the wider al-Qaida movement was surprisingly active, with loosely affiliated groups engaged in actions across the world. Some of these were apparently countered, including reported plans to attack US embassies in Paris and Rome and major attacks against diplomatic and financial centres in Singapore, but others went ahead.

In March 2002, a Christian church in the diplomatic district of Islamabad was attacked, killing five people and wounding 46, and the following month a synagogue in Djerba in Tunisia was bombed, killing 14 German tourists and seven Tunisians and injuring 24. In May, 11 French naval technicians and three Pakistanis were killed and 23 people were injured in the bombing of a coach in Karachi, and the following month the US consulate in the same city was attacked, killing 11 people and injuring at least 45. More attacks followed later in the year, with a suicide attack on the oil tanker *Limburg*, off the coast of Yemen in October. That month also saw the bombing of the Sari night-club in Bali, killing 202 people, including 88 Australians, and injuring 300. While most of the foreigners killed were Australians, the nightclub was often a venue for US service personnel on leave. Finally, in November there were twin attacks in Kenya. In the first, an attempt was made to shoot down an Israeli tourist jet after it had taken off from Mombasa airport. That failed, but a bombing attack on the Paradise Hotel at Kikambala north of Mombasa the same day killed 11 people and injured 50. The hotel was popular with Israelis.

In one sense, these widely spread attacks illustrated the remarkably dispersed nature of the al-Qaida movement and its many associates, some of them with only the loosest of connections. This gave the lie to the idea that the movement was in retreat, but one of the major changes might well have been that it was not even hierarchical and narrowly structured to the extent that might have been the case prior to 9/11. The widespread nature of the actions was also a reflection of the extent of the anti-American mood and of the possibility of organizing attacks on US and other western groups. Furthermore, the extensive Israeli actions against Palestinian groups on the West Bank, especially the systematic destruction of much of the Palestinian Authority's infrastructure during April and May 2002, was widely covered by satellite TV news channels across the Middle East and beyond. While European governments responded critically, if privately, to the Israeli actions, there was little condemnation from Washington, further fuelling support for radical Islamist groups.

On to Baghdad

In spite of the continuing violence in Afghanistan and the evidence of continued activity by a dispersed al-Qaida movement, by the latter part of 2002 almost all of the attention of the Bush administration was on the requirement to terminate the Saddam Hussein regime in Iraq. With a build-up of US military forces in the region, there was a suspicion that war might come early in the winter of 2002–3. While there was a widespread assumption that this was then delayed by the need to gather significant support at the United Nations, there were strong indications that much more practical matters were at the root of delay into the New Year. Put bluntly, the rate of use of a wide range of munitions in Afghanistan in the last three months of 2001, and the continuous use of air strikes in 2002, meant that there was an urgent need to replenish stocks before an assault on Iraq could be contemplated. For much of 2002, US arms companies were working 24/7 to build up stocks for a war that eventually started in late March the following year. It was a war with clear-cut aims: it would involve the liberation of the country from a tyrannical regime, the troops would be seen as liberators not occupiers and the end result would be a pro-western Iraq that would perhaps represent an even bigger success for the war on terror than Afghanistan.

CHAPTER FIVE

Baghdad and Beyond

Introduction

Following President Bush's State of the Union address in January 2002, the focus in Washington moved rapidly towards terminating the Sadam Hussein regime in Iraq. By March 2002 and in the immediate wake of the State of the Union address, the focus was already on the axis of evil, in spite of the sporadic yet intense instances of conflict in Afghanistan. All three axis members, Iraq, Iran and North Korea, caused deep concern. All were developing weapons of mass destruction and all were said to be supporting international terrorism, even if the North Korean support was indirect. Of these, Iran was the really major issue. This was the country that was the focus of the axis of evil, even if it had fought a long and bitter war with another member, neighbouring Iraq. There was, though, a belief that regime change in a country such as Iran would not be easy. With a population of over seventy million, considerable oil wealth and an apparently stable theocratic regime, Iran presented the United States with substantial problems. In one sense, this made regime termination in Iraq a particularly attractive option. 'The road to Tehran runs through Baghdad' was a phrase common in Washington at the time, with a successful regime change in Iraq likely to ensure a compliant Iran.

The antagonism towards the Tehran regime remained deep-seated, not least in the State Department, with the experience of the 1979–81 hostage crisis still relevant (see chapter 1). Even so, Iraq was the more immediate threat, even if it had been seen as a very useful ally in the 1980s, serving as a bulwark against revolutionary Iran. The Saddam Hussein regime had survived its eviction from Kuwait, the subsequent Shi'ite and Kurdish revolts, the air exclusion zones and several coup attempts. By the end of the 1990s, the United States therefore already faced an oppositional Iran and a maverick Iraq that was no longer an ally. There were also doubts as to the stability of the House of Saud. Since these three countries alone controlled close to half of the world's oil reserves, it was not an acceptable proposition to have them outside US influence.

Writing in early 2007, there is something of a consensus that Iraq 'went wrong' because of an almost total concentration on the immediate military campaign at the expense of post-war planning. In this line of thinking, the narrative is one of complete expectation of success. An overwhelming 'shock and awe' air campaign might well have brought the regime to its knees within a matter of days but, if not, a rapid ground invasion would have sealed its fate. Beyond that, though, there was an assumption that coalition forces would be welcomed as liberators and could quickly withdraw, that Iraq would rapidly transit to a functioning free market state that was a very useful ally of the United States and that the end result would be an early success for the New American Century.

The key element here is the view that the US policy-makers did not have substantive plans for Iraq and that this is why Washington 'lost the plot'. In other words, the project was viable and had every chance of success, but the execution was lacking. The view that it would all happen with ease is, in this narrative, pervasive, and a consequence is that blame lies in the detail of execution, not the vision. It is a narrative that is, in practice, warped and even incorporates some rewriting of history. The more accurate narrative is that, from the very start of the war, there were many indications that the process of regime termination itself was flawed. The very idea that the United States could lead a coalition to occupy and reshape a significant Arab state was a gross misreading of regional politics, culture and religion. What were in reality firm plans for post-regime Iraq were predicated on a faulty understanding both of Iraqi governance and of the reaction to foreign intervention by a powerful minority of the population and of wider regional opinion.

In terms of governance, the very process of the first three weeks of the war involved regime termination and not regime change. The system of governance and administration in Iraq was already severely weakened in March 2003 by the effect of many years of sanctions, economic difficulties, the loss of many technocrats and the stultifying effects of a rigid autocracy seeking to hold on to power. Destruction of the centre of that system immediately left a vacuum, especially the loss of control of public order. There were wholly inadequate occupying forces and criminality immediately took root, not least in the wholesale looting of public property.

Three weeks revisited

The key point, though, is that while this happened in the period immediately after the three-week process of regime termination, this actual period already provided abundant evidence that there would be strong opposition to occupation. What was largely missed at the time was an understanding of three aspects of that intensive three-week war: the disposition of Iraqi forces, the immediate problems of urban warfare and the issues of supply line vulnerabilities being experienced even before the Saddam Hussein regime was terminated.

On the first of these issues, most of the ordinary elements of the Iraqi Army were poorly trained and ill-equipped, few of them took part in the fighting and many deserted. Above them were two groups of more elite forces. One was the Republican Guard, which had existed in eight-division strength at the time of the 1991 war but was somewhat diminished by 2003, mainly because of doubts over its loyalty. As a result, Republican Guard units were deployed primarily to the south and east of Baghdad as an outer defensive shield against US Army and Marine Corps forces moving towards the capital from the south east. These forces were exposed to formidable firepower, especially multiple-launch rockets systems and cluster munitions, and suffered thousands of deaths.

In practice, though, these were not the key forces available to the regime, since a reorganization in the 1990s had resulted in the creation of a four-brigade force of the Special Republican Guard, numbering around 20,000 troops and highly loyal. There were, in addition, other units, some of brigade strength, attached to the several branches of the Iraqi intelligence and security agencies. While these Iraqi force structures were reasonably understood by coalition intelligence units, there was an assumption that the elite forces would act as the real defence of the regime. In the event, they did not. Apart from some intense fighting around the international airport, there was little resistance to the US forces as they proceeded to occupy Baghdad in early April 2003. As far as can be understood, virtually all of the regime's elite forces melted away in a process not that far removed from the Taliban actions in Afghanistan nearly eighteen months earlier.

Whether these actions were due in part to the bribing of leading officers, whether they were planned by the regime to provide a basis for post-war resistance or whether many of the officers recognized the futility of direct combat with US forces is difficult to assess, but the key point is that they did not fight. Moreover, the old regime had ensured that massive quantities of munitions were available in many dumps located across central and northern Iraq, with these available to fuel the insurgency. At the actual point of regime termination, the Iraqi Information Minister became known in the western media as 'Comical Ali' because of his insistence that the war was not over. His statement that after the occupation began 'we will bury you' was greeted with nothing less than derision in the west. In practice, the survival of well-trained elite Iraqi Special Forces and abundant quantities of munitions would help form the basis for just such an outcome. Moreover, the very existence of massive quantities of munitions in many different sites gave some indication of the stability of the Saddam Hussein regime and the potential for later resistance. At least in central Iraq, this was a regime that was so confident in the loyalty of much of the population that it could disperse munitions that could have been readily turned against it.

The second aspect of that first three weeks was the immediate experience of urban warfare. This was most noticeable right at the beginning of the coalition troop movements across the border from Kuwait into south-east Iraq. There was immediate resistance in towns close to the border, especially the main port of Umm Qasr which took several days to occupy. This was highly unexpected, given that south-east Iraq was primarily Shi'ite and was expected to welcome the foreign forces. Even so, this aspect of the conflict was largely ignored by most analysts as the main body of the US forces moved towards Baghdad through open country, largely avoiding the towns and cities while making full use of their mobility.

Even so, as those forces moved towards Baghdad, the third factor came into play – supply lines became extended and were immediately subject to persistent attack, so much so that very substantial defensive forces had to be set aside in order to maintain the security of supply. During this period, US forces first experienced a suicide attack. By the third week of the war, with US forces moving rapidly towards the centre of Baghdad, it proved necessary to divert the equivalent of three brigades of troops to the task of protecting the supply lines against attack. This represented close to one third of all the troops available to the United States. Meanwhile, the British forces had still not fully occupied Basra, even though the pre-war expectation had been that this largely Shi'ite city would welcome the British presence.

When the Saddam Hussein statue came down at the end of three weeks, it appeared symbolic of the end of the regime, with huge satisfaction in the United States and, eventually, President Bush's 'mission accomplished' speech on 1 May. Post-war plans included the establishment of four military bases, one close to Baghdad, two near the northern and south-ern oilfields and one towards the Syrian border.[1] These would not have large troop deployments but would be capable of rapid reinforcement. The US military presence was expected to halve within six months to around 70,000 troops, with an eventual force of perhaps 20,000 left in the country.

After a short period of control by General Jay Garner, Paul Bremer came in as head of the Coalition Provisional Authority. He was answerable to Donald Rumsfeld at the Pentagon rather than the State Department; his administration and he pro-ceeded to plan for an Iraq that would be modelled on an ideal free market, including rapid privatization of state assets, a minimum of financial and business regulation, a flat-rate tax system and the use of oil revenues in rebuilding. Iraq would make the transition to a free market untrammelled by restric-tive social legislation and would be a beacon of free enterprise democracy with enduring links to the United States. By May 2003, this was truly expected to be the outcome, in spite of the problems of public disorder and the beginnings of an insur-gency. Only by July and August of that year, and especially with the failure of the killing of Uday and Qusay Hussein to curb the insurgency and the subsequent bombing of the UN offices in Baghdad, was it apparent that the American dream for Iraq was dissipating.

During the course of the following four years, a complex insurgency developed, overlaid by an evolving sectarian conflict. On many occasions, US military and political leaders spoke of substantive progress. In September 2003, there was a firm declaration that the insurgency was down to a few extended families and they were being monitored and constrained. Three months later, Saddam Hussein's detention was expected to end the insurgency, as was the handover to an interim Iraqi administration the following June. Later in 2004, the insurgency was said to be centred on Fallujah, and the takeover of that city in November was expected to remove the core insurgent elements. Elections in 2005 and 2006 were expected to have a positive impact.

None of these expectations were fulfilled. By early 2007, the most conservative estimate of civilian deaths in Iraq exceeded 65,000. Other sources gave much higher figures, exceeding 100,000.[2] A US military source indicated that around 120,000 insurgent suspects had been arrested since the start of the war and that, early in 2007, 27,000 were being detained. Another 20,000 had been killed, yet more insurgents were being recruited.[3] Estimates of the strength of the insurgency after four years of war varied between 20,000 and 100,000,[4] holding down around 400,000 personnel in security forces including US and coalition troops, Iraqi Army and police personnel and many tens of thousands of private security guards. President Bush had said in 2003 that Iraq was a valuable killing ground for terrorists, 'bring 'em on' being the relevant phrase. The crude 'flypaper theory' dictated that Iraq would be the flypaper bringing terrorists (flies) to the country where they would be mired in conflict and eliminated by the US Army and Marine Corps (the insecticide). The war on terror would be

usefully conducted 6,000 miles away from the United States.
Instead, US troops became the flies.

In the United States, domestic opposition to the war finally
became significant in the summer of 2005, and by late 2006
was sufficiently strong to affect the mid-sessional elections
to Congress, giving the Democrats control of both Houses.
There was, for the first time, serious discussion of failure and
withdrawal.

Even though the developments in Iraq in the first four years
of the war were complex and multifaceted, it is useful to isolate
five issues that aid an understanding of the American predicament four years into the war. They are the plans laid by the
Coalition Provisional Authority to maintain influence in an
apparently independent Iraq, the failure to expand the coalition, especially the refusal of India to commit troops, the significance of the Fallujah assault, the nature of US military
casualties and the involvement of Israeli forces. Each illumi-
nates an aspect of the Iraq disaster, and all of them relate to the
predicament of the United States after four years of war and
the possible consequences in the years ahead.

The CPA legacy

Perhaps the clearest indication of the intentions of the
Coalition Provisional Authority, and a relevant counter to the
idea that the occupation of Iraq was unplanned, was the series
of arrangements in place at the time that the CPA handed over
to an interim Iraqi administration in June 2004. The new
Prime Minister, Iyad Allawi, was appointed by Paul Bremer,
along with two key posts of national security adviser and head
of national intelligence. Both of these were five-year appointments and would remain in post whatever government might
take power after subsequent national elections. Furthermore,
before Mr Bremer's departure, a series of edicts were put into

effect placing his nominees as inspectors-general in every Iraqi government ministry, also for five-year terms, and a seven-member electoral law commission was established which would have the power to disqualify political parties. One contemporary analysis concluded: 'In short, a US-appointed prime minister with previous CIA links heads a cabinet that includes several members holding US citizenship, and oversees an administration permeated by a "shadow" inspectorate secured by the departing CPA chief.'[5]

With the ending of the Coalition Provisional Authority, Mr Bremer returned to Washington just as the newly appointed Ambassador to Iraq, John Negroponte, arrived to establish what was intended to be the largest embassy of any country, anywhere in the world. The US Embassy was allocated $480 million in construction costs both for the main complex in Baghdad and for a series of regional missions. Close to 1,000 Americans would be stationed, supported by 700 local staff, with four missions in Mosul, Kirkuk, Hilla and Basra and five further regional diplomatic teams. Some 200 advisers would work with Iraqi ministries.

From a US perspective, such close control of the evolving Iraqi administration was entirely reasonable, given the huge investment made in terminating the Saddam Hussein regime and subsequently endeavouring to combat an evolving insurgency. To others in the region it appeared much more like setting up a client regime beholden to the United States. The counter-argument was that, in a matter of months, or a very few years at most, an elected Iraqi government would be in a position to exercise independence, and the post-CPA arrangements were purely temporary. In practice, such views were treated with deep suspicion in Iraq, partly because of the major investments being made in the US Embassy in Baghdad, as well as the five-year terms imposed on key appointments. Furthermore, the insurgency itself meant that any Iraqi government, whether sympathetic to the United States or not, would remain thoroughly dependent on US military power for its survival. The likelihood of a future government exercising real independence was almost entirely discounted across the region, as was the notion that the war subsequently 'went wrong' for the United States because of a lack of foresight.

The Indian refusal

The problems experienced in Iraq in the first year of the war are encapsulated in the relationship between the United States and India. In the two months after President Bush made his 'mission accomplished' speech, the security situation in Iraq got rapidly worse, with coalition forces facing a developing insurgency and the Coalition Provisional Authority having difficulty in imposing any kind of political order. By July 2003, the United States was looking to extend the coalition by encouraging other countries to commit troops to the cause. It was not difficult to persuade close allies to deploy small numbers of troops, and this had a political value in enabling the Bush administration to point to a substantial multinational endeavour. The difficulty, though, was that large numbers of small deployments, often less than a thousand troops, resulted in substantial problems of logistics and coordination.

What was needed was the willingness of at least one more powerful state to commit a substantial body of troops for six months and preferably much longer. This would take the pressure off US forces in the field, enabling them to concentrate on the major areas of the insurgency, especially Baghdad and the provinces to the north and west. In particular, what would have been most welcome would have been the commitment of a full division, at least 15,000 personnel, from a country able to supply well-trained and disciplined troops, to the Kurdish regions of Iraq in the north east. The reality was that very few countries had the ability to do this and most were ruled out for political reasons.

To deploy a full division in a foreign country and maintain the force through internal rotation requires a very large army – one that can spare close to 40,000 troops without hindering its primary national security functions. Only a handful of countries can do this, especially if they are required to provide full backup including such things as adequate medical support and interpreters. This may seem surprising, given the annual world military budget of over a trillion dollars, but the reality is that most countries have armed forces that are primarily orientated to homeland defence and internal order rather than expeditionary warfare. This includes major regional powers such as Mexico and Brazil. By July 2003, it was already clear that deploying to Iraq was not an issue of straightforward peace-keeping but required combat troops with full support. The countries in a position to offer such forces were few in number. They included Britain, France, Germany, Turkey, Russia, Pakistan, India, and possibly Japan and China. Egypt and Syria were also in the frame because of their proximity to Iraq and their regional knowledge. Both had contributed divisions to the 1991 war, but in 2003 Syria was regarded in Washington as a lesser member of the axis of evil and therefore unacceptable, and the Egyptian government was deeply reluctant to become involved in another Arab state, especially as armed opposition to what was seen as a US occupation was already evident.

Of the other states, Britain was already committed and France and Germany did not have the political will or domestic support to contribute. Turkey was unacceptable to the Kurds and Russia to Washington, even if its disorganized and under-funded army could have actually taken on the deployment. China might have had the military capability but its presence would have aroused huge opposition in Republican circles in the United States, and Japan's armed forces, though substantial, are very much geared to homeland security rather than large-scale distant deployments. A Japanese deployment on this scale would have required a substantial change of emphasis, even if feasible, and it would have been against potentially strong domestic opposition.

While Pakistan might have had the capability, it was already facing problems of instability and loss of control in districts close to the Afghanistan border such as North and South Waziristan. Moreover, the continuing tension with India may have eased since 2000, and Pakistan was receiving aid from the United States in order to consolidate the alliance in the war on terror, but there was still an underlying unease at the prospect of releasing such a large body of troops for an overseas deployment when facing a far more powerful India in an unresolved conflict.

Thus, India was the one country that might make a real difference in Iraq. The Bush administration therefore asked if a full Indian division, numbering 17,000 troops including supporting elements, could be made available. This could take over the security of the whole of north-east Iraq, principally the Kurdish majority areas, where tensions were relatively low. The problem was the Indian domestic environment, even if the government of Mr Atal Behari Vajpayee might gain three substantial benefits by agreeing to the deployment. One was the value in being an ally of the world's only superpower at a time when Pakistan was working hard to position itself alongside the United States in its war on terror. The second was that Gulf oil reserves were becoming increasingly important to India as dependence on imported oil rose rapidly, so an Indian military presence was attractive. Finally, there was a strategic value in being able to project and sustain a full army division overseas, since it would be a deployment that would be watched closely in Beijing. It would be in the heart of the Persian Gulf, a region in which China had sought persistently to develop economic relations with Iran and other oil suppliers.

The problem for Mr Vajpayee was that the Iraq War was thoroughly unpopular in India and his administration was facing important elections in five states later in the year, with a general election due the following year. Opinion polls were showing opposition to the war ranging from 69 to 87 per cent and the state elections were likely to be affected by any decision to deploy troops. Furthermore, the results would be likely to influence the result of the general election. As a consequence largely of these domestic factors, the Indian government refused the US request, despite strong pressure from Washington. In the months that followed, the Indian decision meant that the United States was increasingly bearing the brunt of the conflict. Britain continued its support, as did a number of other countries at a much lower level of involvement, but the prospects for a true coalition involving significant forces other than those of the United States disappeared with the Indian decision. Within a year, the Iraq War was essentially being fought by the United States against insurgents.

The Indian decision was far more significant than seen by most analysts at the time. If the Indian Army had deployed in force, the United States would have been genuinely able to claim that it was leading a worldwide coalition of the willing, countries such as Japan might have put in substantially more troops than they actually did and it might even have been possible to have modest deployments from a number of Moslem countries. Public opinion in India would not allow this, and later claims by Washington of broadly based support sounded increasingly hollow.

Israeli involvement

The Indian decision attracted relatively little attention in the United States and Western Europe, even if it marked the end of any prospect of a substantive international coalition. At the same time, it left one other state to increase its involvement substantially in a move which attracted even less attention outside the Middle East but had even more significance regionally. This was the progressively increasing involvement of Israel in US efforts to control the growing insurgency in Iraq.

US–Israeli defence cooperation stretches back to the early 1960s, a period when the rise of Arab nationalism and closer Arab links with the Soviet Union meant that the US increasingly saw Israel as a regional bastion against Soviet influence. Prior to the early 1960s, most of Israel's arms imports had come from Britain and France, but that changed rapidly, with in particular US aid coming during the Yom Kippur–Ramadan War of 1973. After that, and especially after the loss of the other main regional ally, the Shah's Iran, Israel's significance grew further. It survived the ending of the Cold War and the disappearance of the Soviet threat, not least because of the growth of support for Israel in the United States that arose from the influence of Christian Zionism (see chapter 1).

By the late 1990s, much of Israel's most modern military equipment was American, including new models of the F-15 and F-16 multi-role aircraft, and many advanced projects were essentially joint programmes with US companies, most notably the Arrow anti-ballistic missile system. By the early 2000s, Israel had also gained extensive experience in controlling revolts in the occupied territories, developing tactics and equipment that were appropriate to low-intensity warfare. Although Israel's earlier experience of such warfare in southern Lebanon in the 1980s had not been encouraging, leading to a withdrawal from most occupied territory by 1985, the experience was highly relevant to the later attempts to control the Al-Aqsa intifada that followed Arial Sharon's entry into Haram al Sharif (Temple Mount) in September 2000.

By September 2003, it was obvious that the United States and its limited number of coalition partners were facing a developing insurgency that was proving very difficult to counter. The killing of Sadam Hussein's two sons, Uday and Qusay, in Mosul in July had had no effect on the insurgency, and the bombing of the UN headquarters and the Jordanian consulate in Baghdad shortly afterwards was clear proof that security was not being maintained. It was under these circumstances that relations between the US and Israeli armed forces and defence industries became much closer with the US Army particularly anxious to utilize Israeli experience.

From 1 to 5 December 2003, the head of the Israeli Ground Forces Command, Major-General Yiftah Ron-Tal, hosted a series of meetings and visits from a US Army team headed by General Kevin Byrnes, Commander of the US Army's Training and Doctrine Command (TRADOC). Other members of the US team were Major-General Robert Mixon Jr., Deputy Commander of TRADOC's Futures Center, and Brigadier-General Benjamin Freakley, Commander of the US Army's Infantry School at Fort Benning, Georgia. According to *Defense News*: 'the goals were twofold: to strengthen cooperation among US and Israeli ground forces in future warfighting and military modernization planning, and to evaluate ways in which the US military can benefit from operational lessons Israel has accrued during the past 38 months in its ongoing urban, low-intensity conflict with Palestinian militants.'[6] Quoting a US military source, the journal continued:

> Israel has much to offer in the technological realm, while operationally, there are obvious parallels between Israel's experiences over the past three years in the West Bank and Gaza and our own post-offensive operations in Iraq. We'd be remiss if we didn't make a supreme effort to seek out commonalities and see how we might be able to incorporate some of that Israeli knowledge into our plans.[7]

In a subsequent meeting in March 2004, the Israeli Ground Forces Command staged an event to demonstrate systems developed to defeat Palestinian militias, with US participation including staff from Special Operations Command, the Marine Corp's warfighting laboratory and the Army's National Ground Intelligence Center. US interest included the purchase of the Israeli Hunter robotic reconnaissance aircraft and the evaluation of a wall-breaching variant of an Israeli grenade launcher and an anti-sniper system.[8]

The US Department of Defense's Combating Terrorism Technology Support Office was reported to have ordered some prototypes of a new multi-function sensor for counter-insurgency operations. The ODF Optronics sensor, about the size of a tennis ball, contains movement sensors, microphones, transmitters and speakers enabling it to hear and even communicate with opponents. A major from the Marine Corp's warfighting laboratory commented: 'The Israelis are way ahead of others in some very interesting niche fields.'[9]

From the perspective of the US armed forces, working with the Israelis made great sense. Israel had been working to control insurgencies and paramilitary actions in southern Lebanon and the occupied territories for many years. While the extent of their success was highly variable, the depth of their experience was evident. With the United States losing hundreds of people and having thousands wounded, benefiting from Israeli experience and using relevant equipment was a duty as well as pragmatic.

From the perspective of Arab–Islamic opinion across the Middle East, it was stark confirmation of what the more propagandistic elements were repeatedly saying – the war in Iraq was a neo-Christian–Zionist crusade directed at one of the heartland states of the Arab world. The Israel–US connection is accepted as entirely reasonable across much of American domestic opinion, even if the closeness of the military relationship is virtually unknown. What is almost entirely unrecognized is the systematic and persistent effect this has on wider international opinion, especially but not only in the Middle East. Even less recognized is the huge value this gives to the al-Qaida movement and its associates. A narrative can be maintained of an aggressive neo-Christian–Zionist threat that even transcends the political and social problems endemic to the region.[10]

Fallujah

In November 2004, in the wake of the US assault on the city of Fallujah, experienced Arab analysts pointed to Fallujah as being 'our 9/11'. Such a comment seemed extraordinary if not outrageous to most western politicians and commentators. It was immediately discounted as being little more than extreme propaganda and in the following years the issue of Fallujah and its aftermath disappeared largely from view. In practice, though, the experience of this particular city in the first two years of the war encapsulates much of the experience of the whole Iraq War and offers a lasting explanation of the depth and resilience of the insurgency being faced by the United States.

In the first year of the war, the city of Fallujah had presented considerable problems for the US military because of its development as a centre of insurgent actions. This had been aided by the killing of a number of civilians by US forces early in the war, but the situation escalated in April 2004 following the destruction of a Marine Corps armoured personnel carrier with the loss of five lives on 31 March. On the same day, four US civilian security personnel were killed and their bodies mutilated and burnt by an angry crowd, and there followed several weeks of conflict between insurgents and US Marines. US military commanders were determined to gain control of the city but this did not prove possible, and agreements were eventually made with local leaders. During the fighting, local medical sources estimated that there were several hundred civilians killed and many more hundreds injured.

For the United States armed forces, the crowded city of Fallujah, with its narrow streets and even narrower alleyways, was one of the most difficult areas of conflict in the whole of Iraq. Insurgents were embedded in the city and had substantial support and US service personnel took many casualties. At the same time, the insurgents were armed principally with light weapons, including assault rifles, rocket-propelled grenades, improvised explosive devices (IEDs) and some mortars. The US forces, on the other hand, had a wide range of weapons right through to artillery, tanks, helicopter gunships and strike aircraft.

One single incident in Fallujah illustrates the almost inevitable results of such asymmetry and the political consequences. On 13 April, a Marine Corps supply convoy was ambushed in the city and some vehicles became isolated from the main column. They came under heavy attack from insurgents, seventeen Marines took refuge in buildings, and a large force of Marines, including four tanks, was sent to their aid. A three-hour gun battle ensued, with the Marines bringing in strike aircraft for support, and all the embattled Marines were rescued, some of them wounded. One local commander reflected the Corp's ethos when he said 'This is a story about heroes. It shows the tenacity of the Marines and their fierce loyalty to each other. They were absolutely unwilling to leave their brother Marines behind.'[11]

Within the context of a difficult urban insurgency, this is very much what might be expected – a strong ethos of mutual help in the face of unexpectedly fierce opposition. It may also have been the case that insurgent groups, seeing themselves as fighting an occupying force, would have similarly high motivation. What is more relevant, though, is the subsequent US military reaction. According to the *Washington Post*, just before dawn the following day, 'AC-130 Spectre gunships launched a devastating punitive raid over a six-block area around the spot where the convoy was attacked, firing dozens of artillery shells that shook the city and lit up the sky. Marine officials said the area was virtually destroyed and that no further insurgent activity has been seen there.'[12]

Again, it should be emphasized that such operations were seen by the US military as appropriate responses to insurgents who were more commonly described as terrorists and who were killing and maiming young American soldiers and Marines, but this response was not one of engaging insurgents who were attacking US troops; this was a punitive raid carried out many hours after the beleaguered Marines had been rescued. In the event, this and other operations did not bring the city under control, and the uneasy truce that was agreed in April meant that in the following months Fallujah came to be seen as the main focus of the whole insurgency.

Given that many other parts of Iraq including Baghdad were becoming mired in conflict during the middle of 2004, it is not easy to understand the remarkable emphasis given to Fallujah as the main insurgency centre by the autumn of that year. It is certainly the case that such an emphasis, combined with clear statements that Fallujah would shortly come under US control, had a political value in the run up to the US presidential election in November. The Iraq War had not yet become a central issue in US domestic politics but was still a matter of increasing controversy – a focus on one insurgency centre, and the prospect of its termination, could give the impression that the war was at least being fought on American terms.

In the three months to mid-October, US forces lost over 200 people killed and well over a thousand wounded in the insurgency across Iraq. With Fallujah seen as the key to defeating the insurgents, around 15,000 Army and Marine Corps troops were assembled for the assault, compared with just 4,000 Marines available at the time of the earlier April conflict. The main tactics employed were steady advances into the dense urban environment, using substantial force to destroy any element of resistance. Tanks, artillery, helicopters, AC-130 gunships and strike aircraft were all used, leading to widespread destruction in the 'city of mosques'.

After three weeks, the city was under the control of US and Iraqi government forces, but the destruction was massive and there were reliable reports of several thousand people killed and half the 39,000 buildings in the city destroyed or badly damaged. US military sources reported that the insurgents had borne the brunt of the casualties because most of the inhabitants of the city had left before the assault got fully under way. Doubts were cast on this evaluation because nearly a third of the 1,450 suspected insurgents detained were quickly released as non-combatants, even though almost all those detained were young men of military age. The suspicion, widely confirmed by local Iraqi sources, was that most of the casualties were civilians. Moreover, even as the assault on Fallujah was under way, major insurgent activity broke out in Mosul, requiring the US military to divert 2,400 troops to maintain security there. Even after Fallujah had been brought under coalition control, ringed with roadblocks and with extensive searches of people and vehicles, the city quickly became a centre for the production of roadside bombs.

The Fallujah assault in November 2004 was expected to be the turning point in the war for the United States, but it had little impact on the insurgency, which intensified in the following year. Instead, its impact was of quite a different order to that anticipated in Washington. Because domestic politics required a high-profile example of US capabilities in Iraq, extensive facilities were made available to the US media to cover the operation. As a consequence, there was graphic television coverage, from behind and within American lines, of the very high levels of firepower being used. It was intended and served as a vivid demonstration of American capabilities and a warning to opposing forces. To audiences across the Middle East and the wider Islamic world, however, the effect was the opposite. Instead, the coverage was proof of a violent and determined occupying power that would wreck a city in the pursuit of its aims. Moreover, the regional satellite news channels such as Al-Jazeera and Al-Arabiya provided graphic coverage of the effects of the assault, especially in terms of civilian casualties. It was, once again, an indication of the remarkably different outlooks in public opinion in the United States and most of the Middle East. To the United States, Fallujah was a proof of capability, even if its success in terms of the war was brief. To much of the Islamic world, it was a 9/11.

Casualties and morale

The nature and range of US casualties and the impact on troop behaviour and domestic opinion is a significant feature of the evolution of the war, as is the much larger number of Iraqi casualties. In the first four years of the war, the US military lost 3,240 killed and 24,500 injured, a ratio of dead to wounded of nearly 1:8. This compares with most modern wars where the ratio is 1:3. In Vietnam it was 1:2.6. Reasons for this include substantial improvements in the development of body armour, battlefield medicine and the rapid evacuation of casualties. It is not that more soldiers are getting wounded, it is that far more of the wounded are surviving. Most of those with serious injuries are moved rapidly to a military hospital at Ramstein in Germany and then on to the Walter Reed Army Hospital in Washington.

Because of the use of body armour and the standards of treatment aiding battlefield survival, it is more likely that, where there is serious injury, it will be to limbs, the groin, neck and face, and many of those wounded suffer lifelong effects. Furthermore, it is now recognized that non-lethal exposure to blast has an effect on the brain even if there are no visible external signs. Developments in neurological research coupled with recent experience in Iraq are beginning to explain the basis of what was previously termed 'shell shock', a phenomenon now thought to result from direct physical effects on the brain and to have long-term health consequences. In the case of Iraq, this is now believed to be affecting many thousands of veterans.[13]

The effect of the large number of casualties on domestic opinion was not immediately apparent since the Bush administration was at pains to minimize any public reference to returning casualties. Visits by political leaders to hospital wards were rare and the press was discouraged from covering the return of coffins. Over the period 2005–7, though, the accumulation of reports in the local press and broadcast media did much to bring home to domestic communities the impact of the war. Including non-combat injuries and physical and mental illness, it is estimated that over 40,000 troops had been evacuated from Iraq back to the United States by early 2007, meaning that most towns and city districts had what amounted to personal experience of the consequences of the war.

The effects on troop morale and behaviour are also difficult to quantify but there is abundant evidence that the circumstances in which the young men and women found themselves were at least partly responsible for their conduct under fire, two factors being particularly important. One was the sheer uncertainty of counter-insurgency operations against unseen opponents in urban environments, with the constant risk of death or serious, often crippling, injury. The other was the availability to the US troops of extraordinarily high levels of firepower, with an almost inevitable tendency to use that fire-power in response to any perceived or actual hostile action, whatever the civilian consequences. This is an explanation, not a condoning, of the behaviour, but has to be recognized as a reality dictated by the nature of the war and of its environment. The punitive raid in Fallujah cited above is just one of many examples from Iraq, but most contemporary conflicts, including the Russians in Chechnya and the Israelis in Lebanon, have involved similar instances. The difference for the United States in Iraq has been the persistent and very widespread coverage of such actions. They may go largely unreported in the western media but get intensive coverage in the broadcast and print media across the Middle East.

Four years on

As the war moved into its fifth year, the conflict became increasingly complex. On the coalition side, the great majority of the forces were American and Iraqi with few other countries apart from Britain making much of a contribution. In spite of four years of training, much of the Iraqi police force was regarded as unreliable and beholden to particular militias, and there remained endemic problems of absenteeism and incompetence in the army. Although the level of discipline and control within the army was much higher than in the police force, it was drawn primarily from Shi'a and Kurdish communities and was widely seen within the Sunni community as an instrument of external control.

At the root of the violence were three identifiable elements. One was a criminal entity, often organized into quite substantial and well-armed groups and prone in particular to kidnapping and robbery for profit. A second was an insurgency that was itself complicated. It was drawn in part from neo-Ba'athists, former soldiers and nationalists, but also involved foreign paramilitaries who were loosely affiliated to the wider al-Qaida movement. A tendency within the insurgency was for a greater embracing of fundamental forms of Islam, with this enhanced by the presence of dedicated foreign jihadists. Even by the second year of the war, Iraq was a combat training zone for such paramilitaries. To the al-Qaida movement, this was very much more valuable than the Afghanistan war against the Soviet Union in the 1980s had been for an earlier generation. That was a mainly rural war fought largely against badly trained and poorly motivated conscripts, whereas in Iraq the paramilitary groups could hone their skills against well-equipped professional soldiers in an urban environment. By the start of the fifth year, there was some evidence that more Iraqis were supporting the broad aims of the al-Qaida movement rather than being primarily concerned with defeating the US occupying forces.

The third group was made up of militias attached to Shi'a political parties, including the Mahdi Army and SCIRI (Supreme Council for the Islamic Revolution in Iraq). While these and other groups had a function of protecting Shi'a communities, there was also a strong element of opposition to the American military presence. Nevertheless, the extent of sectarian violence was such that there were close to two million internally displaced refugees in Iraq, in addition to the two million that had left the country, with many of the casualties being caused by such violence rather than the insurgency and the forceful coalition attempts to control it.

One further factor was that the elected Iraqi government was not only very weak but had a high proportion of its membership drawn from former exiles. Their willingness to work together was limited partly by the complex nature of the violence, but also by a strong tendency to safeguard their own positions, with little commitment to forging a more united state.[14]

Conclusion

The predicament of the United States in Iraq has resulted in numerous analyses of what went wrong, most of them focusing on the United States and some involving a degree of self-justification, having been written by early participants in the endeavour, especially some of those associated with the original Coalition Provisional Authority. Few of the accounts have concentrated on the predicament of Iraq – the appalling human costs including the vast numbers of civilian casualties, the four million refugees (more than one in seven of the entire population) and the failures of reconstruction. On any independent assessment, the quality of life in Iraq was actually far worse four years into the war than even under the brutal autocracy of Saddam Hussein.

By 2007, three justifications were emerging among the war's supporters in the United States. One was that the insurgency was almost entirely due to the activities of al-Qaida and, as a consequence, Iraq remained the core focus for the entire war on terror. Although this was a misleading and dangerous simplification, it served the purpose of linking the war back to the 9/11 atrocities. A second was the claimed role of Iran in fostering sectarian violence, thereby making the connection between the war in Iraq and the country regarded by neoconservatives and others as the primary actor in the axis of evil. This, too, was hugely misleading, given that the more important of the Shi'a militia groups, the Mahdi militia owing allegiance to Moqtada al-Sadr, had relatively poor relations with Tehran. Even so, it served a purpose in providing an explanation for the continuing problems of a costly war. Finally, blame could be levelled at the Iraqis themselves. The political leadership turned out to be inefficient, deeply sectarian and corrupt, presiding over sectarian divisions that verged on civil war. This was perhaps the most useful complaint in that it implied a

degree of sheer ingratitude on the part of a political establishment and an Iraqi people that had been delivered from a
dictatorship and now refused to govern with appropriate
authority.

In one sense this takes us right back to the idea that regime
termination in Iraq may have been correct but that the problems have stemmed from the execution of the process, not
the fundamental policy. If there had been more coalition
troops, if the Iraqi Army had not been sent home and if de-
Ba'athification had been less extreme, then Iraq would have
been liberated and could have been guided into an easy if not
inevitable transition to a markedly pro-western free-market
democracy. The Iraqis might have had to be taught a lot by an
essentially benign United States but they would have learnt.
Moreover, with a continuing US military presence, Iraq would
have been the key component in ensuring the longer-term
security of the Persian Gulf as the region's geo-strategic importance increased. Problems of potential instability in Saudi
Arabia would be of less concern and, above all, Iran would be
compliant. With pro-American administrations in Kabul and
Baghdad, Iranian influence would be much diminished and
any regime in Tehran would recognize the futility of opposition to the world's sole superpower that was so completely
entrenched in the region.

All this would have followed from successful regime termination in Iraq, and it would have been successful had it been
executed with greater intelligence. The problem with this outlook, which is likely to endure in Washington whatever the
eventual outcome in Iraq, is that it is so fundamentally flawed
as to be delusional. In some ways it harks back to the extraordinary attitude of the Eden administration in Britain at the
time of the Suez crisis in 1956. Nasser and his nationalization
of the Suez Canal was seen by Anthony Eden almost as a
reincarnation of Hitler and a fundamental obstacle to British

influence, not just in the Middle East but across much of Asia. As a result, an extraordinary and entirely misjudged late colonial military expedition was mounted that failed almost as soon as it started, undercut by a United States that was not prepared to see its own interests compromised.

The Iraq operation was a delusion because it presumed that a foreign power could simply terminate a regime in a major Arab state and replace it with an acceptable regime of its own choosing. Moreover, this was a foreign power that was closely linked to Israel, a relationship that had an enduring negative resonance across the region. Operation Enduring Freedom was flawed from the outset and would, in all probability, not have succeeded whatever the manner of its execution. Above all, it was 'a war too far' in that it inserted a foreign power, perceived as a neo-Christian crusader, into the heart of the Islamic world at a time when radical Islamists centred on the al-Qaida movement could hardly have asked for anything more likely to aid their cause.[15]

PART III

Consequences

CHAPTER SIX

Towards the Long War

Introduction

As the war on terror moves towards the end of its first decade, there is a strong argument that this is a conflict that will evolve over some decades rather than mere years. There has been a marked tendency to describe it as the 'Long War Against Islamofascism', a term that was promoted with some force as the Bush administration ran into increasing local opposition to its policies during 2006. In this outlook, 9/11, al-Qaida, Hizbullah, Hamas, the insurgents in Iraq, the Taliban in Afghanistan, and al-Qaida and other radicals in Pakistan are all subsumed into a single entity – terroristic Islamofascism – which is the gravest threat to western civilization. An alternative analysis sees the war on terror as substantively counter-productive to western security interests and potentially destabilizing in terms of wider issues of global security.

For a conflict to have the potential to last two or three decades, there have to be powerful motives on both sides to engage in such a war, coupled with persuasive reasons why neither of the opposing sides will be able to achieve dominance or be willing to retreat from their respective aims. This chapter provides a brief overview of the evolution of the al-Qaida movement, with particular emphasis on its eventual aims and the timescale over which it hopes to achieve those aims. It then examines those aspects of western policy that may suggest an engagement with a very lengthy conflict before making some suggestions as to what alternative policies, developed primarily by the United States and its closest coalition partners, might provide another approach for responding to Islamic radicalism. Finally, the chapter seeks to assess the likelihood of such changes being introduced.

Bin Laden and al-Qaida

Although the term al-Qaida ('the base') only began to come into common usage in the late 1990s, it appears to have originally been used in the early 1980s to describe a hostel in Peshawar in Pakistan used to house young Arab jihadists preparing to aid the mujahideen in the fight against Soviet forces in Afghanistan. The hostel was established by the young Osama bin Laden who arrived in Peshawar in 1980 aged 23. In the early 1980s, he was closely linked with the Pakistani Inter-Services Intelligence, a singularly powerful security and intelligence agency that vigorously pursued Pakistan's policy of gaining influence in Afghanistan.

Facing competition from a much more powerful and stronger India, Pakistan had tended to ally itself with China, in contrast to India's closer links with the Soviet Union, but the Soviet invasion of Afghanistan meant that Pakistan was effectively on the Cold War front line. It was therefore in a good position to gain support from the United States, with substantial aid and armaments flowing from the CIA and other US government agencies through Pakistan into Afghanistan, frequently via the ISI. Osama bin Laden himself was regarded as a CIA asset, although his skills were more in the areas of logistics and construction rather than combat.

His own background and personal wealth stemmed from his father, who had risen from being a Yemeni labourer to run one of the most powerful construction companies in Saudi Arabia, leaving a fortune estimated at $11 billion in 1968.[1]

Given that this was before Saudi Arabia had gained its immense oil riches, bin Laden's father had had a truly remarkable career. His son studied business and management at university in Jeddah in the late 1970s but was much influenced when taking courses in Islamic studies taught by Muhmmad Qtub and Abdallah Azzam. Qtub was the younger brother of Sayyid Qtub, the radical Egyptian Islamist who had been tortured and killed by the Egyptian authorities in 1966 and is now regarded as one of the most significant radical Islamic thinkers of the mid-twentieth century. He was opposed both to the pervasive western influence and economic control in the Arab world in the post-war era and specifically to the relatively secular Arab nationalism of the Nasser era.[2]

Bin Laden worked in his father's company after an unsuccessful university career and went to Pakistan and Afghanistan, working with Azzam in the burgeoning campaign against the Soviet occupiers in Kabul. Throughout much of the 1980s, bin Laden worked tirelessly to build up logistic support for the mujahideen but also took part in combat. He and other organizers had copious amounts of money, principally from Saudi Arabia and the United States, the latter channelled mainly through the CIA. When the Soviet Union finally pulled out of Afghanistan in 1989, bin Laden and others saw that defeat as a clear example of the rightness of their cause, but external support rapidly dried up. Many fighters returned to their own countries, including bin Laden to Saudi Arabia where he offered his services to the royal family in the wake of the Iraqi occupation of Kuwait in August 1990 and its perceived threat to the Kingdom.

The decision of the House of Saud to allow a massive western force to enter the Kingdom in order to evict the Iraqis was a shock to bin Laden and many like him. The Soviet aggressors had been evicted from an Islamic country, Afghanistan, by an extraordinary force of guerrilla freedom fighters, yet the most important land in Islam was now allowing in crusader forces to protect it. Furthermore, Saudi Arabia was seen to be under threat from the secular regime of Saddam Hussein. Just as Sayyid Qtub had bitterly opposed Nasser's secular nationalism from inside Egypt, so Saddam Hussein should be opposed by right-minded fighters who had just humbled one of the world's two superpowers. Instead, the other superpower, a Christian crusader entity with the closest of connections to Zionist Israel, was being allowed untrammelled access to the Kingdom of the Two Holy Places.

While some Saudi religious scholars approved of the US intervention because of the need to safeguard the Kingdom, others did not and many were arrested or harassed. After a period under house arrest, bin Laden moved to Sudan for five years but was forced to leave in 1996. This was largely because of pressure on the Khartoum authorities from the United States and Egypt following an assassination attempt on the Egyptian president, Hosni Mubarak, that was traced back to groups in Sudan. Bin Laden and his group then moved back to Afghanistan, taking refuge in the Tora Bora region. In September of that year, the Taliban militias, with substantial Pakistani support, captured Kabul and in the following two years imposed a rigid but stable Islamist rule on much of the country.

Even by 1998, though, they were still engaged in a bitter civil war with a disparate group of largely non-Pashtun warlords later known as the Northern Alliance. Bin Laden and the al-Qaida group rapidly built up a network of training centres, attracting paramilitaries from across South-West Asia and North Africa. The primary purpose of the centres was to assemble and train fighters to aid the Taliban in completing their control of Afghanistan, but the longer-term intention of the al-Qaida movement was to extend its ambitions to embrace a religious revolution across the Islamic world, always within the context of abiding opposition to crusader–Zionist influence. By the late 1990s, examples of direct action extended beyond the earlier attempt to assassinate Mubarak to include attacks on US military units in Saudi Arabia and the bombing of US embassies in Kenya and Tanzania.

Al-Qaida aims

While western representations of the al-Qaida movement are frequently crude to the extent of seeing its supporters as unthinking extremists devoid of political aims, this is very far from reality. While there was substantial dispersal of the movement, and an evolution after 2001 away from a more narrow and centrally directed entity of the late 1990s, the movement has clear-cut aims directed at two principal sets of opponents, the 'near enemy' of unacceptable regimes in Islamic countries across much of the Middle East and beyond, and the 'far enemy' centred on the United States but involving its close allies such as Britain.

Before exploring the several short-term and long-term aims of the movement, it is worth examining the status of Israel in the al-Qaida world-view because it is more complex than might be expected. From a perspective across the Arab world, the existence of Israel and its development into a singularly powerful and nuclear-armed state is a constant affront. Israel's success in the Six Day War, its avoidance of defeat in 1973 and its steady takeover of the West Bank is bad enough, but its control of the third most holy site in Islam, Jerusalem, is a continuing reminder of powerlessness. Israel's reversals in Lebanon hardly count for much in this context, and its extraordinarily close relationship with the United States only adds to the radical Islamist view that those elite rulers of Islamic states that remain close to the United States are to be opposed with a particular vehemence.

The al-Qaida movement has long opposed the existence of the State of Israel and this has been a theme in bin Laden's statements for a decade or more. It has not, though, been a central feature and it is only in the past five years that the Palestinian cause has been embraced as a key aspect of al-Qaida's aims. The reason for this has much to do with one of the main original support bases for al-Qaida coming from within Saudi Arabia and other west Gulf states where support for the Palestinian cause has never been especially strong. During the 1950s and 1960s, many hundreds of thousands of Palestinians in refugee camps across the West Bank, Gaza, Jordan, Syria and Lebanon took refuge in education, and many went on to form an educated diaspora that spread across the Middle East and even Europe and North America. In countries such as Saudi Arabia and the Gulf emirates, they were highly significant in the utilization of oil wealth in the 1970s and 1980s, sometimes forming the backbone of public services in areas such as medicine, education and public administration.

Yasser Arafat's support for Saddam Hussein in 1991 was substantially unhelpful but this was only exacerbating a frustration among young men within Saudi Arabia and elsewhere that too many jobs were held by Palestinians. Through no fault of their own, Palestinians were regarded as unfair foreign competitors and it made little sense for the al-Qaida movement to highlight the wider Palestinian plight too much. At the same time, across the Middle East, Israel was seen as anathema, and by the time the hard-line policies of the Sharon administration were having their effect in the early 2000s, al-Qaida became far more prepared to embrace the Palestinian cause.

Beyond support for Palestinians, a support that many if not most Palestinians eschew, the al-Qaida movement has a range of short-term aims. The first is the eviction of the crusader forces of the far enemy from the Middle East, with the eviction of American forces from Saudi Arabia being a dominant aim of the late 1990s and early 2000s. It has to be remembered that al-Qaida developed as a movement, with widespread support, largely because of this affront of having substantial US forces permanently based in the Kingdom of the Two Holy Places after the 1991 Gulf War. It was the military presence at places such as Dhahran, and later at the Prince Sultan Airbase, that was the key issue, much more than the tens of thousands of American civilians that worked in Saudi Arabia for oil companies and other organizations. It was almost certainly the Saudi government's perception of this undercurrent of opposition that made it prevent the US Air Force using Saudi airbases for the Desert Fox operation against Iraq in 1988 (see chapter 2).

From al-Qaida's perspective, it successfully achieved its aim of forcing the US armed forces to leave Saudi Arabia when the Prince Sultan base was turned over to care and maintenance after the withdrawal of over 4,000 USAF personnel in 2003–4. This Air Force decision may have seemed surprising in view of the importance of Saudi Arabia to the United States but it was an indication that the US State Department fully recognized the significance of the US military presence in boosting the radical Islamist cause. Nevertheless, in spite of this perceived victory, the al-Qaida movement sees this as no more than a first step in evicting the crusader forces from right across the Middle East.

A further core aim of the movement is the termination of the House of Saud as the unacceptable, corrupt, elitist and deeply pro-western Keeper of the Two Holy Places and its replacement by an acceptable form of genuine Islamic governance. This aim, though, is complex and its implementation has varied. At times in recent years there have been attempts to weaken the Saudi economy through attacks on western oil companies and even on major oil installations, the attempted bombing of the Abqaiq oil processing plant near Dhahran in February 2006 being a notable example. There have also been persistent attempts to destabilize the Kingdom through internal opposition. At other times, though, the tactics appear more to have revolved around a form of 'entryism' – seeking to promote change through the rise of cohorts of advisers and opinion formers within the ruling elite. Whether change is achieved through a violent process or by such a process of transition is less important, though, than the requirement to bring about the replacement of the House of Saud.

Regime change in Saudi Arabia is just one aspect of the much wider requirement for terminating regimes across the region. The traditional lead candidate for such change after Saudi Arabia is Egypt, with Jordan and Gulf Emirates also in the frame. Further afield, Pakistan has long been seen as a state with the potential for violent regime change but it has been pushed to one side in recent years by the potential for change in Afghanistan and Iraq. In many ways these two countries are now seen as the lead contenders for a realistic possibility of establishing the al-Qaida ideal of Islamist governance, although Pakistan remains very much in the frame.

Beyond the Middle East and South-West Asia, the al-Qaida movement sees firm links with radical paramilitary groups in many other countries including Indonesia and Chechnya. Perhaps the most notable example is the indirect support for Islamic separatists in southern Thailand, where a bitter conflict has evolved in recent years. The military takeover in Bangkok in 2006 involved, surprisingly, an attempt to conciliate the separatists, but the early indications are that the separatists are so disparate and the conflict so deeply embedded that this will be both protracted and difficult.

Beyond these five main aims – eviction of crusader forces, termination of the House of Saud, replacement of other regimes, support for Palestine and for separatist movements elsewhere – the al-Qaida movement has the much broader aim of the re-establishment of some form of Islamist Caliphate. In some senses, this harks back to the well-developed Caliphates of the early Islamic period, especially the Abbasids, but it involves both an idealized representation of such an era and the belief that a new Caliphate would be far more Islamist than almost anything on offer at present. The Abbasid Caliphate, particularly in its early years, was a remarkable era in the evolution of world civilization. Around 800 to 900 AD (in the western calendar), it covered much of the Middle East and encompassed a veritable flowering of medicine, the sciences, art, literature and architecture. It was relatively liberal in its treatment of Jewish, Christian and other minorities and was, in its time, the world's most advanced civilization. A Caliphate in the al-Qaida mould would be a very different entity.

A question of timetables

Two of the most significant aspects of the war on terror concern the nature of the al-Qaida movement and the timescales within which it operates. Throughout this book, the term 'al-Qaida *movement*' is used in order to help avoid the idea that this is a narrowly hierarchical organization with a single leader who is firmly in control of a worldwide paramilitary movement. This has never been the case, even in the late 1990s, although there was then a sense in which there was more direction from a central group than there has been since. Even then, though, al-Qaida was much more of a network of interconnected groups. Those responsible for the 9/11 attacks certainly had close links with bin Laden and others in the higher echelons of the movement, but key members had developed their ideas largely while living in Germany. After 9/11, though, the movement became much more dispersed and might best be described as something between a franchise, a consortium or even a network of networks.

What is at least significant, though, is the question of timescales. The al-Qaida movement is not in the business of short-term success. It has evolved over a period of perhaps a decade and a half but anticipates that its shorter-term aims may take decades to achieve. That it has evicted the US forces from Saudi Arabia is a useful first step, that it sees the crusader enemy hopelessly mired in Iraq and Afghanistan is even better, but these are positive developments in a much longer process. The decades of the 2010s and 2020s are those to which al-Qaida looks for achieving some of its further aims, so that a forty-year time period from the mid-1990s is considered to be the appropriate frame of reference. The much greater aim of the evolution of a radically new Islamist Caliphate may take many more years to achieve – somewhere between fifty and a hundred years.

This necessarily means that key figures such as bin Laden and Zawahiri do not expect to see all their aims achieved, and this is an attitude that will permeate many of the dedicated supporters of the movement. From their perspective, though, the early years of the movement are proving to be highly successful, with the United States' involvement in Iraq being their greatest single asset. What is worth recognizing here is that this eschatological perspective makes al-Qaida different from many secular revolutionary movements. With such movements there has tended to be the confident expectation that success could be achieved in the lifetimes of the revolutionaries. The al-Qaida movement is simultaneously revolutionary and deeply religious; early success has less importance.

Al-Qaida after 2002

Although there was a presumption that the al-Qaida movement had been dispersed and seriously damaged by the loss of its bases in Afghanistan, as chapter 4 showed, associates in a number of countries continued to be active, even if some of the attacks had little to do with any centrally planned operations. In addition to attacks in Tunisia, Kenya, Pakistan and Indonesia, there was an attempt to destroy the *Limburg* oil tanker off the coast of Yemen and reported attempts to attack targets in France, Italy and Singapore.

Even so, there was a sufficient presumption of success within the Bush administration that it was fully appropriate to proceed with regime termination in Iraq. Following Bush's State of the Union address in January 2002, the administration had clearly extended its war on terror to encompass unacceptable regimes, and the assumed decline of al-Qaida meant that it would now further diminish as many of its more senior figures were killed or detained. Although bin Laden and Zawahiri remained at large and the Taliban leader, Mullah Omar was still free, the status of al-Qaida and the Taliban was considered to be so low that the war on terror could now move on to Iraq and, possibly, Iran.

While it is reasonable to conclude that the al-Qaida movement was more constrained from mid-2002 onwards, attacks that were at least indirectly related to its aims continued at a high level of intensity. Indeed, in the five years after the 9/11 attacks, the movement was far more active across the world than in the five years prior to those atrocities. In 2003, for example, there were four major sets of attacks, leaving aside the development of the insurgency in Iraq and the continuing violence in Afghanistan.

In May 2003, there were four bomb attacks in Casablanca against targets linked to western countries or commercial interests, killing 39 people and injuring 60. That same month, there were multiple bombings of western compounds in Riyadh, killing 29 and injuring 200. Three months later, a US target in Djakarta, the Marriott Hotel, was bombed, killing 13 and injuring 149. Finally, in November 2003, two double bombings were carried out in Istanbul. In the first of these, two synagogues were attacked, killing 24 people and injuring 255. Shortly afterwards, two British centres were the focus of two more bombs in Istanbul. One was aimed at the British consulate in the city and the second at the offices of the HSBC Bank. Twenty-seven people were killed in these attacks, including the British Consul and his personal assistant, and 400 were injured.

During 2004, there were yet more attacks, primarily against western or Israeli targets. In March 2004, there were multiple bomb attacks against commuter trains in Madrid, killing nearly 200 people and injuring over 1,000, and that same month saw two attacks in the Uzbekistan capital of Tashkent, killing 19 people and injuring 26. Many of those killed and injured were police officers. While these attacks related partly to domestic circumstances, four months later there were attempts to attack the US and Israeli embassies in the same city. In September 2004, there was another attack on a western target in Djakarta. This time it was the Australian Embassy, representing a country that was fulsome in its support for the Bush administration. Eleven people were killed and 161 injured. Finally, in October 2004, Israeli tourists were once again the focus of attacks in Sinai. The Taba Hilton and a camp site at Nueba, both in Sinai, were bombed, killing 34 and injuring 122.

In 2005, there were multiple bombings in London, Sharm al Sheikh and Amman, and further attacks in Bali, an attempted missile attack on the USS Kersage amphibious warfare ship in Aqaba harbour and a bomb attack on a high security government office district of Karachi. The following year, the Egyptian Red Sea resort of Dahab was bombed, a US diplomat was killed in a bomb attack on the US consulate in Karachi and attempts were made to bomb the US Embassy in

Damascus and the massive Abqaiq oil-processing plant in Saudi Arabia. In early 2007, the focus moved to Algeria with attacks on police stations in the east of the country and on the Office of the Prime Minister in Algiers.

This list does not include some of the more loosely connected attacks, nor the many interceptions of planned attacks. More significantly, it does not even begin to take account of the huge range of attacks by numerous jihadist groups in Iraq and Afghanistan. If these are included, then the increase in the intensity of operations by the movement in the mid-2000s is around sixfold compared with the start of the decade.

A number of factors help explain the resilience of the movement and its expanding support, most of them concerned with the manner of the conduct of the war on terror. Before addressing those, however, it is worth recognizing the importance of developments in western Pakistan. While the Musharraf regime in Islamabad is assumed to be an ally of the United States in its war against al-Qaida, the reality is a much more complex set of relationships, many of them conditioned by the attitude of successive Pakistani governments to Afghanistan. Faced with a far more powerful country (India) to the east, and with the intensely disputed territory of Kashmir a constant source of friction, Pakistan has seen its influence in Afghanistan as a key adjunct to its regional status.

In the 1980s, Pakistan sought to counter India's significance in the South Asia region in two main ways. One was to maintain good relations with China, effectively balancing India's long-term relationship with the Soviet Union, and the other was to act as a conduit and agent for the United States in its support for Afghan rebels opposing the Soviet occupation of the 1980s. After the Soviet withdrawal at the end of the 1980s, elements within the Pakistani military, especially the powerful Inter-Services Intelligence (ISI) agency, saw great value in aiding the Taliban movement in its progressive takeover of Afghanistan.[3] This meant that after 9/11, Pakistan was in the difficult position of needing to be allied to the United States while losing its considerable influence in Kabul once the Taliban regime had been terminated. Moreover, the Pashtun support base of the Taliban extended well into western Pakistan, especially frontier districts such as North and South Waziristan. In walking the tightrope between governmental support for the United States and popular opposition to US operations in the region, Musharraf has had to be especially careful about confronting pro-Taliban and pro-al-Qaida groups across much of western Pakistan.

In spite of opposition from the Bush administration, the compromise has been to effectively cede central control of key border districts to local communities, however much they might allow free activity of radical paramilitary groups. Two important consequences of this are that Taliban elements operating in Afghanistan have been greatly helped in terms of logistics, training and support in districts across the border, and the al-Qaida movement has effectively had a substantial area from which it could operate. While this has not been on the scale of the freedom of movement in Afghanistan in the late 1990s, it has enabled the movement to redevelop its existing connections to like-minded groups across the world and to develop and enhance new links.[4]

Support for the movement

From a wide range of polling evidence and other research, it is apparent that support for the broad aims of the al-Qaida movement has increased substantially since 9/11, and especially since the termination of the Saddam Hussein regime in Iraq and the subsequent development of the insurgency. The reasons for the increasing support are several, and there are also clear synergisms at work. In looking at the longer-term prospects for the movement, and given that it is operating on a decades-long timescale, it is worth examining the factors and their interrelationships.

Two substantial issues are casualties and detentions, with these relating very much to media developments. On the question of casualties, western military forces have been deeply reluctant to undertake 'body-counts', especially of civilians, but sufficient data is available to show that the war on terror has so far resulted in the deaths of civilians on a level that is massively higher than the original 9/11 atrocities. In Afghanistan over the past seven years, there have been at least 10,000 deaths but the figures for Iraq are very much higher, at least 70,000 for the first four years and probably much higher, with well over 100,000 injured and close to four million refugees.

On the matter of detentions and prisoner abuse, it is difficult to obtain accurate figures, but a consensus view would be of around 100,000 people detained for varying lengths of time from September 2001 through to late 2006, with at least 15,000 detained at any one time. Most of these detentions were with no prospect of a trial under any internationally recognized judicial system and while most were in Iraq and Afghanistan, they include some thousands across the world, not least in the United States and Britain. Again, figures may be imprecise but reports in early 2006 suggested that, by that time, barely 1,000 detainees had been brought to trial with 500 acquitted. It is certainly possible that many of these figures are underestimates, with one March 2007 report indicating 27,000 suspected insurgent detainees in Iraq alone and 120,000 people detained for varying lengths of time in the first four years.[5] There has, furthermore, been the endemic problem of prisoner abuse, renditions and torture, with the Abu Ghraib issue being a small part of an overall problem.

For convinced supporters of the war on terror, especially in the United States, the casualties and detentions are an inevitable part of the conduct of a war against a dangerous and determined opponent, but the effect on wider opinion, especially among the world's Islamic communities, is almost entirely unrecognized. Furthermore, this links with highly relevant changes in the operation of the international media. Central to these has been the development of effective regional satellite TV news channels, such as the Qatar-based al-Jazeera station and the Dubai al-Arabiya channel, that provide detailed coverage, often hour-by-hour, of the conflicts in Iraq and Afghanistan. Al-Arabiya now broadcasts via seven satellites, giving it a footprint across the region and beyond; evening news broadcasts are watched by up to 20 million people. Al-Jazeera has even larger audiences across the Middle East and South-West Asia but also reaches into communities beyond the region, extending now to a global English-language service. Although facing increasing competition, al-Jazeera remains the leading Arab-language channel, combining professional technical standards with graphic coverage of events.

This coverage, which is from a markedly different outlook from that of CNN, let alone Fox News, has had a profound effect on knowledge of events in the region, especially as they relate to casualties, detentions, abuse and torture. Furthermore, it is supplemented by an extraordinary range of overtly propagandistic material emanating from numerous jihadists groups in Iraq, Afghanistan, Pakistan and many other countries. Using various combinations of audio- and video-cassettes, DVDs, broadband internet links and other forms of data transmission, including mobile phones, there has evolved what amounts to a virtual environment encompassing world-views that are radically different to those of western governments and the media outlets that reflect them.

There is no sign of any likely diminishing of the influence of this environment – if anything its significance is likely to grow further, with attempts by the United States and its coalition partners to provide an effective counter-narrative so far proving almost entirely inadequate.

The Israel factor

Although Palestinians are frequently reluctant to find their predicament supported by the al-Qaida movement, it is certainly the case that Israel's control of Jerusalem and its actions in the occupied territories have been of enduring value to the movement. There may be a strong argument that Israel's dominance is a consistent diversion for Arab and Islamic opinion, being blamed for many problems that are actually internal to neighbouring states. Even if this is far from true, it still contributes to the wider narrative of the al-Qaida movement of Islam under threat and of the need for a jihadist conception of a renewed Caliphate to counter this threat.

Israel is, in practice, a hugely valuable focus for the movement, and its involvement in Iraq has attracted far more attention across the region at a time when it is almost unknown in the United States and Western Europe. The point here is that it is possible to erect a crude narrative that the termination of the Saddam Hussein regime in Iraq was essentially a process of a neo-Christian crusader force, centred on a superpower 6,000 miles away, destroying an Arab state in a process involving Zionist expansionism. Moreover, the aim is to maintain long-term influence and control over the oil resources of the Persian Gulf. Even more potent is the idea that this Crusader–Zionist force has developed a power base for an occupation that is centred on the ancient city of Baghdad, the original seat of the Abbasid Caliphate which was the most notable and effective example of Islamic rule in the entire history of Islam.

Iraq and jihad

While the Iraqi insurgency is complex and multifaceted, draws from many sectors of Iraqi society and is further complicated by sectarian violence, a significant aspect of it has been the involvement of foreign paramilitaries. At times their importance has been exaggerated by the Bush administration in order to connect an increasingly unpopular war with the 9/11 attacks and the wider global war on terror. Two to three years into the war, foreign paramilitaries accounted for less than a tenth of suspected insurgent detainees, but they have certainly been significant in at least three respects. One has been the willingness of many of them to engage in suicide missions, a second has been that many others have gained combat experience and taken that on to other theatres of conflict including Afghanistan, and a third has been the spread of insurgent technologies.

Most foreign paramilitaries have espoused the overall aims of the al-Qaida movement, being concerned with regime change across the region and the withdrawal of the forces of the far enemy and its coalition partners. At the same time, and given al-Qaida's very long timescale of action, Iraq is potentially of immense value as a combat training zone, with the ability to create new generations of jihadists with experience of advanced urban guerrilla warfare. In one sense, this is in contrast to the aim of most Iraqi insurgents who have the primary ambition of defeating US forces. Most neo-Ba'athist and nationalist insurgents want the Americans out of Iraq immediately, but the al-Qaida movement would prefer the US troops to remain in Iraq for many years. Over that whole period, the movement would be able to train cohorts for longer-term action against both the far and near enemies, the United States and its partners on the one hand and illegitimate elitist regimes on the other. This is a process likely to unfold over decades.

Although this divergence of aims has not been resolved, two developments in late 2006 and early 2007 were relevant. One was that US intelligence sources believed that more Iraqi nationals were joining the loose group of insurgents allied to the al-Qaida movement in Iraq, and the second was that in many towns and cities under insurgent control there was a marked move towards rigid religious observance. In both ways, therefore, there was a sense in which a relatively secular society was embracing a sense of jihad which might transcend the immediate desire of evicting the 'crusader' forces, seeing paramilitary opposition to the US military forces in Iraq as part of a much longer-term project. If this analysis is correct, then the Iraq War is of huge value to the eventual aims of the al-Qaida movement, for whom the longer it lasts the better.

The view from Washington

When President George W. Bush moved to his summer residence near Crawford, Texas, in 2005, the mother of a young soldier killed in Iraq, Cindy Sheehan, pitched camp on an approach road as a protest against the war. During the course of the next few weeks she attracted opprobrium from some local residents but an increasing amount of support, some from the immediate neighbourhood but much more from a wider community across the United States as the local, regional and eventually national media took up the story. In taking this unusual step, she unexpectedly acted as a focus for a steady increase in opposition to the war that had previously been lacking. It was not an anti-war movement as such, but more a perceptible change in public mood as the war continued with little apparent chance of success.

In addition to the mounting costs and the almost perpetually bad news coming out of Iraq, the other major contributing factor to the anti-war mood was the steadily increasing numbers of military deaths and serious injuries. These received little federal attention but even by mid-2005 involved well over 10,000 deaths and injuries, many of the latter being evacuated back to the United States suffering life-changing after-effects. The awareness of these human costs, permeated through American society largely by way of the local media, did much to enhance the growing opposition to the war, which came to a head in the campaigns for the mid-sessional elections to Congress in November 2006. While there were other factors involved, including some scandals in the Republican Party, the growing opposition to the war was a significant issue in the loss of both Houses of Congress to the Democrats.

Such a change would seem to suggest that a major revision of the war on terror might be in prospect, not just in terms of military involvements in Iraq and Afghanistan but also in respect of wider activities in Yemen, the Horn of Africa and elsewhere. There are reasons to doubt that possibility, not least because there remains a profound belief on the political right that the war on terror, in all its forms, is winnable. Furthermore, since the United States is dealing with uncompromising extremists, there is no alternative to a decisive military victory. International terrorism does not inhabit the realm of conventional politics and cannot therefore be addressed as a political problem. Islamofascism is the threat to the United States in particular and the world as a whole. It is a definable entity that includes al-Qaida and its many associates, Hamas, Hezbollah, the Taliban, Pakistani Islamists and all manner of Iraqi insurgents, whether linked to al-Qaida or not. This is an existential threat from an enemy that seeks weapons of mass destruction. That enemy must be destroyed and that can only be achieved through force.

This belief is deeply rooted and extends to a fundamental concern that the American approach to an evolving global society, the New American Century, is the only way forward for the world but is under severe threat. This outlook goes right back to the utter shock of 9/11 – an atrocity that came at a time of great promise for the New American Century project – and a perception that Islamofascism is the major threat to the vision. In September 2001, the 'jungle' bit back, and it has to be tamed. Not using all available force to destroy this enemy threatens not just the security of the United States but the future of the world. It is every bit as dangerous an enemy as the Soviet evil empire of the Cold War years.

Within days of the Democrat victory in the mid-sessional elections in 2006, the Bush administration was accusing Congress of unpatriotic behaviour as support for funding for the war began to erode. It was a charge that was vigorously denied, but the Democrats faced the real difficulty of divisions within their party over the most appropriate policies to be adopted, especially in Iraq. Opinions varied from early to phased withdrawal to staying the course with a heavily modified military posture emphasizing Iraqi capabilities. In the face of such divisions and always willing to use the patriotism issue, supporters of the Iraq War had substantial political advantages, in spite of domestic opposition to the war.

Such an analysis suggests that the next few years will see little change in policy or, if there are changes, these will be presented more as appropriate adjustments to the conduct of the wider war on terror. What is therefore more pertinent is to assess the possibility of more substantial change over the period through to 2015. If the al-Qaida movement is engaged in a decades-long struggle with the perceived enemies of true Islam, will those enemies, and especially the United States, continue to fight in the current mode or will they develop other strategies that might be far more threatening to the intentions of the al-Qaida movement?

As far as the United States is concerned, three of the main areas of focus are Afghanistan, Iraq and oil security. In

Afghanistan, a revitalized Taliban movement has to be defeated to prevent the development of a new safe haven for the al-Qaida movement and its associates. More than this, an Afghanistan that espouses radical independence from the west will also undermine US influence across Central Asia, including the oil-rich regions of the Caspian Basin. It will also aid support for the Islamist movement in Pakistan, and could result in oppositional governments in Kabul and even Islamabad. While NATO's International Security Assistance Force may be encouraged to take the main burden in Afghanistan, there will be real doubts as to its commitment and, in the final analysis, the United States will have to provide the spine, maintaining whatever combat forces are necessary to ensure that Taliban and other militias are excluded from power.

In Iraq, the United States has three options, only one of which is currently acceptable. The first is precipitate withdrawal, but this, in the Republican view, will leave behind a failed state. In such circumstances all likely outcomes are unacceptable. One is that radical jihadists, including the al-Qaida movement, will establish themselves as solid movements with all the logistics and morale to extend their influence in the region, not least in the oil-rich western Gulf states. While they may not take over the entire Iraqi state in the face of a Shi'a majority and Kurdish opposition, they will develop a power base that will be of great value to their long-term plans. If, secondly, there is also a civil war, then the outcome would be highly uncertain but could well involve greatly increased influence for Iran. It is just possible that there could be another outcome – the rapid introduction of a hardline autocratic regime under the control of a Saddam Hussein-like figure. Such a regime could well be friendly to the United States, and could even be as useful as the Saddam Hussein regime was prior to 1990, but this is intensely unpredictable, bearing in mind what happened before.

A second option is the basing of forces in Iraq that are concerned principally with securing the major oilfields and with maintaining a degree of control of the borders. Military deployments to achieve this degree of influence might be centred on a handful of major bases combined with heavy reliance on air power. The cities, in effect, would be left to look after themselves and whatever form of governance emerged in Iraq, either regionally or nationally, would either be dependent for its survival on the US military presence or would at least have to recognize the power that US forces continued to wield.

This is a plausible scenario and there was a tendency towards this option during the early part of 2006. Where it failed, and where it would fail again, is in three different aspects: the ability of insurgents to operate with impunity in many towns, cities and even rural parts of Iraq, the capacity of insurgents to target oil production and delivery systems, and the risk of mounting sectarian violence. In other words, the United States could not maintain the necessary security at one remove, and there is little evidence that an Iraqi government could develop strong enough security forces to maintain control on its own.

Finally, there is the option of staying the course, with appropriate military modifications of which the 'surge' of early 2007 was one example. It is possible that some progress might be made towards achieving the aim of a stable pro-American government in Baghdad, but there are few signs of this happening. Nevertheless, given the probable outcomes of the alternatives, this remains the most likely policy. Moreover, this may be the case whatever the nature of domestic opinion or of future administrations, an aspect that takes us back to the question of oil security.

This book is not in the business of promoting the argument that the termination of the Saddam Hussein regime was primarily about gaining control of Iraq's oil resources. Nor were the investment opportunities available with the privatization of state assets greatly significant. It is more a question of the regional geopolitics of oil in the context of global trends that is significant. As discussed in chapter 3, the three main trends in oil security are, first, that most of the industrialized world has long been dependent on oil imports; secondly, that the United States and China are also becoming rapidly more dependent on oil imports; and, thirdly, most of the remaining oil is in and around the Persian Gulf. In the short term there will be a scramble for the control of African oil reserves and Russia may use its oil-exporting power for a variety of political ends, mainly concerned with regaining an element of great power status after the collapse of the 1990s. Even so, this is not 'where it's at', so to speak. The Persian Gulf is the focus and will remain so.

Consider now a scenario in which the United States admits defeat in Iraq and withdraws. It may choose to maintain large forces in Kuwait and to expand its deployments in Qatar and Oman as well as further building up its bases in Djibouti and Diego Garcia and maintaining an augmented naval presence. But this will all be in the context of an Iraq which is outside its control, an Iran which is rigorously independent and may seek an enhanced regional role including greater influence in Iraq, and a Saudi Arabia of questionable stability. With those three countries containing close to half of all the remaining oil in the world, this is simply not acceptable. Moreover, political realities mean that this applies to any future US administration.

The central problem is that the Bush administration's decision to terminate the regime of Saddam Hussein by invasion and subsequent occupation meant that other options of regime management were ruled out, not just for the mid-2000s, but for the longer term. There was, essentially, a ratchet effect of that decision. Unless there is a fundamental change in US attitudes to the use of oil and the security of its supply, then any US administration is unlikely to contemplate a complete withdrawal from Iraq.

Responding to al-Qaida

There has been a persistent tendency to identify almost all insurgent activity in Iraq as being due to the al-Qaida movement. This may be a substantial exaggeration but the Iraq War has certainly been of great value to the movement, both in terms of widespread support because of some of the bitter consequences of the war such as the civilian casualties, mass detentions, torture and prisoner abuse. This does make the Iraq predicament a key aspect of the influence of the movement, but it is one among several. If it is accepted that the conduct of the war on terror in its first five years proved counter-productive, leaving an unstable Afghanistan, a chaotic Iraq, a transnationally active al-Qaida movement and a strongly anti-American mood across much of the world, what alternative policies might undercut support for the movement?

In addition to legitimate forms of counter-terrorism action, including the disruption of plans, detention, trial and imprisonment of offenders and increases in international cooperation, there are both general and specific approaches that might collectively make some difference. In general terms, these include intensive action to minimize civilian casualties as part of a rapid scaling down of military operations that have so benefited the movement and its loose associates. An ending of detentions without trial and adherence to the Geneva conventions, the ending of prisoner rendition, of torture and abuse and the closure of the Guantanamo complex would all remove hugely significant propaganda advantages currently enjoyed by the movement.

More specifically, action to undercut support for the individual aims of the movement are required. In countries such as Saudi Arabia, Pakistan and Egypt, moves towards more democratic governance and a weakening of the bitter socio-economic divides would be highly significant. A broadly-based resolution of conflicts in the Caucasus, Thailand and the Philippines and a major reconsideration of policies in Afghanistan, including a willingness to engage with opponents, would also undercut support. In particular, the predicament of the Palestinians is a constant source of support for the movement – a resolution of that conflict based on justice would do serious damage to the support for the al-Qaida movement. By no means all of these issues are within the purview of the United States and its coalition partners – many relate to the policies and outlooks of regional governing elites. At the same time, western involvement with, and support for, such elites has been an enduring feature of recent years, and there is much scope for major changes in policy.

The Iraq situation is the most difficult of all, given the experience of the first four years of the war, but there is little alternative to a US withdrawal, whatever the arguments cited earlier. Neither Saudi Arabia nor Iran would welcome the prospect of a bitter Sunni–Shi'a conflict on their borders and there is certainly a case to be made that a US withdrawal would force the conflicting parties within Iraq to come to a political accommodation sooner than might be expected. The Shi'a majority cannot control the country in the face of a determined and well-armed Sunni opposition, but the Sunni minority cannot defeat the majority. Only an accommodation would provide a degree of mutual stability. There is little prospect that long-term US involvement will ever bring stability and a much greater prospect that it will aid al-Qaida in its decades-long intentions. While withdrawal from Iraq might leave an environment in which radical jihadist movements can develop, the continuing presence most certainly is providing a remarkable combat training zone, a situation of immense value to the al-Qaida movement and its vision.

Conclusion

At the time of writing, and moving into the seventh year of the war on terror, there is little prospect of any of these changes in policy. For quite different reasons, the al-Qaida movement and the United States are together locked into a substantive conflict, with little room for change. Against this, the many difficulties being experienced by the United States and its few remaining coalition partners may, at some stage in the next few years, occasion a substantial change in orientation, possibly embracing some of the approaches outlined above. This would represent a major change in the US military outlook of 'taming the jungle' (chapter 2) and of oil security policy (chapter 3). What remains to be discussed is whether the war on terror, and its dominance of the current security outlook, is actually a diversion from other substantive global problems, and whether the evolving failure of that war might make the concept of sustainable security more attractive in the coming years.

CHAPTER SEVEN

Sustainable Security

Business as usual

When Donald Rumsfeld took office as Secretary of Defense in 2001, he brought with him a clear idea of the future direction of US military force. While the military posture would be a key part of the projection of US influence, the make-up of the forces would change substantially. Power would be exercised through the medium of agile high-tech forces, made greatly more efficient by the interconnections enabled by network-centric warfare. There would be a minimal need for 'boots on the ground' with much greater emphasis on precision strike based primarily on air power. There would be a contin-ued emphasis on the need for amphibious forces, and Special Forces would be maintained and enhanced for the many operations that might be required in failed and failing states or other locations where US interests were at risk. In gen-eral terms, though, promoting and safeguarding the New American Century would not require the massive land forces of the Cold War era – the jungle could be tamed not by overall suppression but by isolating individual threats and eliminat-ing them.

One effect of the protracted operations in Afghanistan and Iraq was to render this vision obsolete, but this did not involve a complete rethinking of attitudes to security so much as the development of appropriate modifications. The broad thrust of the changes has been the decision to increase the size of the

US ground forces, both Army and Marine Corps, by 92,000. This will most likely be achieved over about six years but it is not the intention to maintain large ground forces in particular regions outside the United States, at least under normal circumstances. There is a presumption that Iraq and Afghanistan will, in some mysterious way, eventually be resolved, but the longer-term plan reflects the experience of these two wars. As such, it will ensure that the United States does have the ability 'to fight another lengthy irregular war, with units rotating into theatre and training indigenous militaries to carry out missions on their own turf...'[1] Expressing this in more military jargon, the Pentagon's principal Deputy Undersecretary of Defense for Policy, Ryan Henry, pointed out that 'the need to move forward from a force that is garrisoned for highly kinetic, major combat operations to one that has more of its mass back in the United States – but rotates forward – is something we see in the future.'[2]

There is an implication that major lessons must be learnt from Iraq and Afghanistan but this is still in the context of maintaining US military dominance. Such dominance is to be ensured by a combination of very high levels of defence spending, together with a range of new and modified capabilities. Unless a budgetary crisis intervenes, US military spending into the 2010s will be roughly equal to the military spending of all other countries of the world combined, even discounting the direct war costs in Iraq and Afghanistan. Such spending will enable the Pentagon to maintain its full range of global reach capabilities, including the US Navy's carrier battle groups and the Marine Corps's amphibious forces. The US Air Force will maintain its air expeditionary capabilities and, although there may be a further draw-down of forward-based units in Western Europe, selected bases in Eastern Europe and Central Asia will be developed. Furthermore, a unified military command for sub-Saharan Africa, AFRICOM, will be established that will be modelled on CENTCOM and designed to ensure greater US influence at a time of increasing competition for Africa's fuel and mineral resources.

Recognizing the risk of missile proliferation, and the potential limitations of military operations demonstrated by the Scud attacks in the 1991 Iraq War, there will be a renewed emphasis on missile defence, including a priority for theatre defences to protect forward-deployed forces, especially in the Middle East. National missile defence will also be enhanced, including forward-basing in Europe. Some forms of missile defence may involve the development of directed energy weapons utilizing laser and particle beam systems. In terms of weapons theory, directed energy weapons can be said to approximate to 'ideal' weapons in terms of speed and accuracy of delivery of energy to designated targets. The airborne laser that is currently under development is the main example of such a system, with plans for powerful space-based lasers and tactical high-energy lasers also under consideration.[3]

While the US nuclear weapons stockpile has been substantially reduced, some modified systems have already been fielded, such as the B61-11 earth-penetrating warhead for attacking deeply buried targets, and the planned Reliable Replacement Warhead programme is intended to provide robust and versatile weapons for the next several decades. One of the most indicative developments, though, is the intention to modify some long-range missiles by replacing the nuclear warheads with powerful conventional warheads. Combining range, speed and accuracy, such systems could be fired at very short notice, aiming to impact on targets virtually anywhere in the world within perhaps an hour of the order being given, with an initial operational capability being planned for 2009.[4] The thinking behind such a system, known as Prompt Global Strike (PGS), is illustrated very well in the January 2006 *Quadrennial Defense Review*:

> We are shifting from responding after a crisis starts to pre-
> ventative actions so problems do not become crises. We are
> also shifting from a 'one size fits all' deterrence strategy to tai-
> lored deterrence for rogue powers, terrorist networks and
> near-term competitors. PGS would give us the ability to
> respond conventionally to the full range of contingencies –
> 24 hours a day, seven days a week, 365 days a year. That may
> mean we can strike a terrorist cell before they disperse to
> carry out an attack.[5]

Prompt global strike, directed energy weapons, developments in amphibious warfare systems, carrier-based air power,
Special Forces and increases in Army and Marine Corps personnel are all expression of a firm intent to maintain military
dominance – in effect to ensure that the control paradigm is
maintained. In spite of the extensive problems being experienced in Iraq and Afghanistan and the wider difficulties of a
counter-productive strategy in the overall war on terror, these
all indicate that there has been no real change in thinking,
more a degree of modification to respond to short-term difficulties. It is therefore relevant to question the overall outlook of
the US security posture, and indeed that of its allies such as
Britain, in terms of the developing challenges to international
security. If these challenges suggest that this posture is actually
irrelevant, then will the recent disastrous experiences in Iraq
and the more general failure of the war on terror prompt a
change of paradigm?

Global challenges and global responses

Although most military and strategic thinking still relates to
states and terrorist groups as being the major problems for the
future, there are indications that some of the more thoughtful
analysis goes beyond such issues to look at other more significant global trends. In the United States there is now some

concern over the security implications of climate change[6] and the Development, Concepts and Doctrine Centre, a UK Government defence think tank, has published studies on future security trends that put some emphasis on socio-economic divisions and environmental constraints.[7] While these do represent a degree of new thinking, they are essentially focused on maintaining the security of particular states. As such, they concentrate primarily on the responses required to meet threats and maintain security for the states concerned rather than placing an emphasis on preventing the threats developing in the first place.

Taking a more holistic approach to new challenges tends to be mainly concentrated in a few independent think tanks, with some evidence that an approach that is being termed 'sustainable security' is attracting attention.[8] This new thinking focuses on three main trends that are together likely to influence international peace and security over the period through to around 2040: socio-economic divisions, environmental constraints and militarization.[9]

Socio-economic divisions

The period since the collapse of the Soviet Union has seen the global economic system embrace a market economy mode of operation, with centrally planned economies in retreat. Even China has moved towards a mixed economy and the overall result has been reasonably sustained economic growth, sometimes reaching 8–10 per cent per annum increases in per capita GNP. This impressive overall trend is seriously marred in two ways. One is that major regions of the world have not experienced even more modest rates of growth, including most of sub-Saharan Africa, parts of the Middle East and South Asia and significant parts of the former Soviet Union.

The second trend, which is of even greater concern, is that the economic growth that is being achieved is singularly failing to deliver socio-economic justice. What is happening, instead, is that much of the increase in wealth is being excessively concentrated in about one fifth of the global population, with the gap between that group of rather more than a billion people and the remaining 5.5 billion widening steadily. The extent of the socio-economic divide is startling and remains largely unrecognized, as does the fact that it has increased markedly in recent decades. The period from 1965 to 1990 was particularly acute – in 1960 the average GNP per capita for the richest 20 per cent of the world's population was thirty times that of the poorest 20 per cent. By 1995 this had widened to sixty times. More recently, a detailed study from the World Institute for Development Economics Research (WIDER), a research and training centre of the United Nations University, has published an analysis of the global distribution of household wealth. By 2000, the richest 10 per cent of the world owned 85 per cent of household wealth whereas the poorest 50 per cent owned barely 1 per cent of the wealth.[10]

The 'elite' community is very substantial and is not rigidly concentrated in a few geographical areas. While many of the North Atlantic and West Pacific states have most of their populations among this elite, there are substantial wealthy elites in India, China and Brazil, and most southern countries have smaller elites. It is much more of a transnational phenomenon than forty years ago, but the entire process has been accompanied by substantial and greatly welcome improvements in education, literacy and communications among the majority of the world's people. This has been one of the major success stories of international development in recent decades, but it carries with it the implication that it is far easier for marginalized peoples to be more readily aware of their own marginalization. The old idea of a 'revolution of rising expectations' of the consumer society era of the 1970s risks being replaced by a revolution of frustrated expectations.

While the most immediate effect of the brutal divisions of wealth and poverty is continual marginalization, ill-health and suffering, it also leads to insecurity in the form of petty crime or, frequently, a desperate need to migrate in the hope of improved well-being. It can also lead to the development of radical and even extreme social movements, as has been the experience in countries such as Peru, Mexico and Nepal, as well as unexpected reactions in countries experiencing very rapid growth. China has witnessed many thousands of instances of riots and other forms of social unrest in towns, villages and cities away from those few metropolitan centres in which so much of the national growth is concentrated. In India, the quasi-Maoist Naxalite rebellions of the 1970s were thought to have disappeared but they have made a remarkable comeback and now affect a third of all of India's states. While there are many reasons for the development of radical Islamist movements such as al-Qaida, a very strong element is the perception of marginalization.

Overall, this developing response from the margins does not necessarily involve a revolt from the poorest of the poor – more commonly it is to be found among educated people who do not share in the fruits of economic growth. Nor is it true to describe this phenomenon as a single global movement, even though some movements, such as al-Qaida, do have transnational aspects. At the same time, the perception of global inequalities feeds into many radical social movements, as does the belief that a small group of countries, led predominantly by the United States, seeks to maintain the socio-economic status quo. It is probable that the trend towards radical reaction has some similarities to the global anti-colonial movement of the 1940s and 1950s. There was no single tightly organized international movement, but there was a commonality that was pervasive and strengthened individual components. Similarly, as anti-elite movements develop, whether rooted in political, religious, nationalist or racial aspects of human identity, one should expect a certain transnational solidarity to develop, providing considerable empowerment to individual movements.

Environmental constraints

Although the original *Limits to Growth* study of 1971 was widely derided by traditional economists, its central thesis, that the global ecosystem would not be able to handle the increasing impact of human activities within seventy years, has a much greater resonance over thirty-five years later. In terms both of resource depletion and pollution, it is becoming more obvious that the entire biosphere is now subject to human impact. In relation to resources, there may be problems over competition for gems, some high-value minerals and water, but the major issue is oil, with its extraordinary concentration in the Persian Gulf and the increasing dependence of almost every industrialized and industrializing state on imported oil (see chapter 3).

Even more significant as an aspect of environmental constraints on development is the impact of climate change, with a subtle but crucial difference in likely effects now apparent. Until around a decade ago, climate change induced by carbon dioxide and methane releases was expected to have its main impact on relatively wealthy temperate and near-polar latitudes. While the impact might be considerable, these regions had a much greater capacity to adapt and cope than poorer countries of the south. What became clearer from the mid-1990s was that the economically weaker tropical and subtropical regions would also be greatly affected.[11] Three impacts were likely. One would be an increase in the severity of tropical storms, likely to have severe impacts on heavily populated coastal cities and on some of the world's most fertile croplands in major river deltas. The second would be the impact of rising sea levels leading to the inundation of such cities and deltas.

The third would be the most serious of all – a tendency towards a drying out of the tropical and subtropical regions with relatively more rainfall over oceans and polar regions.

The implications of all of these trends on countries badly equipped to adjust and cope would be considerable, but a 'drying out' could be wholly catastrophic. If those land masses that support the majority of the world's 6.5 billion people are likely to dry out over the next thirty to forty years, when the population of these regions is already set to increase substantially, then there will be endemic suffering, frustration, a desperate urge to migrate to more tolerable localities and intense anger if the response of the elite states is to 'close the castle gates'. It is when the trends towards majority marginalization and environmental constraints increasingly interact that we see a combination of factors that will cause a degree of insecurity that will be far greater in scale than any current issue.

What has to be stressed is that this combination involves two very clear trends that have already been sustained for some decades and, at least for now, show no sign of change. The widening wealth–poverty divide and consequent majority marginalization has developed over at least forty years, and climate change has accelerated over a similar period.[12] None of the economic policies currently in existence appear likely to make substantive differences to the wealth–poverty divide, and the responses to climate change, while welcome, remain minimal compared with what is required to curb the trend.

Militarization

Although global military spending fell at the end of the Cold War, mainly because of the collapse of the Soviet military budgets, there was a transformation in the military posture of the United States, and to a lesser extent of allies such as Britain, to a posture focused on maintaining security in a world of disparate threats – a matter of 'taming the jungle' (chapter 2). This trend received an extraordinary boost in the wake of the 9/11 atrocities, leading to enforced regime termination in two countries, and a robust global campaign against the al-Qaida movement. In essence, the response to 9/11 was the rigorous implementation of what might best be termed a control paradigm. It was led initially by the United States, but with support from a number of western countries, although that support has weakened in recent years.

Even so, the vigorous military response has been maintained in the face of intense problems, especially in Iraq but also in Afghanistan, and chapter 6 has put forward arguments to indicate that the control paradigm will not easily be abandoned. In the face of future instability arising out of an environmentally constrained and economically divided world community, including mass migratory pressures and the rise of radical and extreme social movements, that paradigm will result, at least on present trends, in the securitization of these issues and a determined effort to maintain the status quo. Much as the war on terror has emphasized the regaining of control rather than an exploration of the motives and mindsets of radical Islamist movements, together with determined efforts to counter the factors that are ensuring they thrive, so the tendency will be to do likewise in the face of future problems rather than see them as capable of amelioration.

Sustainable security

More than thirty years ago, the economic geographer Edwin Brooks feared a scenario of 'a crowded glowering planet of massive inequalities of wealth, buttressed by stark force yet endlessly threatened by desperate people in the global ghettoes'.[13] While that looks more likely now than it did then, there are numerous changes in policy that can greatly decrease the risk of such a societal dystopia. Reversing the widening socio-economic divisions will require policy changes in three broad areas. One will be comprehensive debt cancellation, given that southern indebtedness remains a persistent obstacle to development in spite of many fine words and some limited action. While there has been much talk at G8 summits and other gatherings, the concrete results have been a pale shadow of what is required. A second will be a wide-ranging reform of north–south trading relations towards a genuine fair trade agenda, reversing those aspects of the world economy that still date largely from the colonial era and have persistently limited the development prospects of the majority of the world's people. Much of this relates to the weak terms of trade of the many southern countries still dependent on primary product exports for much of their foreign exchange earnings. With few exceptions, the major industrialized states have rarely shown genuine interest in the many devices available to enhance prospects for fair trade. Similarly, major importers have been all too ready to encourage the exploitation of cheap labour, often under appalling conditions.

Finally, there is an urgent requirement for direct assistance in developing gendered and sustainable development processes that aid the poorest while being environmentally sound. Much development assistance of recent decades has been concerned much more with the development of new markets for the 'donors'; it has frequently been an overt instrument of foreign policy and has commonly taken the form of loans rather than grants. While recognizing the requirement for competent governance, there remains huge scope for major improvements in the quantity and quality of development assistance.

Preventing the worst effects of climate change will require three forms of action. One is that the main polluters, primarily the industrialized states of the north, will need to cut back carbon emissions to a level far lower than is now envisaged and in a much tighter timescale. Something of the order of 60 per cent cuts by 2020 will be essential, achieved by a combination of huge improvements in the efficiency of energy use and a much higher reliance on renewable energy resources. One major effect of such a change will be a markedly decreased reliance on fossil fuels, including oil. Decreasing the dependence of major industrialized states on Persian Gulf oil will substantially decrease the risk of further conflict in the region. The second form of action is that countries now engaged in industrialization will need to be consistently aided to develop forms of industrialization that have a low environmental impact. There is evidence that leaders in some major industrializing countries, including China, do recognize the potentially disastrous effects of climate change on their own countries. Among other factors, they are reluctant to be more adventurous in reshaping their own industrialization because of fear of a lack of competitiveness and a deep-seated antagonism to being required to respond to a situation created by the existing wealthy industrialized world. If the lead comes from North America and Europe, the prospect for fully multinational action is greatly improved.

Finally, even the most rapid transformation of economies away from current impacts on climate change cannot happen in time to prevent a degree of such change. As a consequence, direct assistance will be required to aid communities in the south as they are forced to respond to some degree of environmental impact, including storm intensity, coastal inundation and persistent drought.

One of the main critiques of the traditionally state-centred approach to international security has been the idea of 'common security' which is predicated on a high level of state cooperation for addressing common problems. It has been paralleled by 'critical security studies' which is more directly critical of the state-centred approach and also embraces an emancipatory agenda, not dissimilar to elements of peace research. In parallel, there has been the development of the 'human security' approach which prioritizes the value of individuals, groups and communities.[14]

Sustainable security does no more than combine elements of the common and human security approaches while ensuring that policies adopted build in a capacity for long-term resilience. In the broadest terms, the combination of socioeconomic divisions and environmental constraints provides a unique circumstance. Unless current trends are reversed, there is a very high probability of exceptional levels of insecurity over the next three decades and beyond. The traditional state-centred approach will be to prioritize maintaining security by military and related means, with inadequate attention to altering the trends. Sustainable security involves adopting the policies outlined above to do just that. The timescale for the required changes is essentially the period through to around 2015.

While there were indications in the late 1990s of a recognition of failings both in free market globalization and environmental impacts, one of the main effects of the 9/11 attacks was to reinforce the control paradigm, setting back by five years or more the possibility of embracing the sustainable security approach. At the same time, the first few years of the war on terror have been notable for the systematic failure of the control paradigm. This therefore provides for the possibility of a rethinking of the paradigm, not just as it applies specifically to the war on terror but also to overall global trends. In one sense it is a contest between a very deeply embedded outlook, supported by some of the world's most powerful lobbies, and a recognition that global security has to be approached in entirely new ways – in effect a paradigm shift.

Two aspects of the current predicament give some cause for optimism. One is the growing awareness of the confluence of environmental constraints and socio-economic divisions as the core drivers of future insecurity. This awareness has increased markedly since 2000 and is reflected in greater support for cooperative international development and a rapidly increasing acceptance of the reality of climate change and its dangers. The second is the palpable failure of current security policies. One of the most powerful inducements for new thinking is that the very approach to the war on terror is increasingly recognized as a lost cause. In an extraordinary way, the deeply mistaken and counter-productive responses to the 9/11 atrocities mean that the possibility of breaking out of the obsolete control paradigm may even be greater than a decade ago. If so, then we are left with an extraordinary opportunity not just to rethink the immediate response to the al-Qaida movement but to go beyond that to reshape our entire approach to global security.

Notes

CHAPTER I THE POLITICAL CONTEXT

1 Operation Eagle Claw on 24 April 1980 was a failed attempt to rescue the hostages. It resulted in the deaths of eight US service personnel when two of the aircraft involved collided.

2 For details of the 'Project for a New American Century', see www.newamericancentury.org; accessed 6 April 2007.

3 *Statement of Principles*, 'Project for a New American Century', 3 June 1997, Washington.

4 Ibid.

5 Ibid.

6 Ibid.

7 Malcolm Dando, *Preventing Biological Warfare: The Failure of American Leadership* (Palgrave Macmillan: Basingstoke, 2002).

8 Charles Krauthammer, 'The Bush Doctrine: ABM, Kyoto and the New American Unilateralism', *The Weekly Standard* (36), 4 June 2001, Washington DC.

9 For a sympathetic discussion of Christian Zionism, see David Brog, *Standing with Israel: Why Christians Support the Jewish State* (Front Line Books: Lake Mary, Florida, 2006).

10 'International Christian Embassy Jerusalem': www.icej.org/; 'Stand for Israel': www.ifcj.org; both accessed 9 June 2007.

11 For a succinct analysis of the development of Christian Zionism, see the work of Donald Wagner, available at www. informationclearinghouse.info/article4959.htm. Another useful source is Steven Sizer, *Christian Zionism: Road Map to Armageddon*, available at www.Christchurch-virginiawater.co.uk/articles/ivp.html; accessed 1 February 2005.

12 For a detailed analysis of the Clinton policy, see Nick Ritchie, 'Containment-plus: Clinton and Iraq at the End of the 1990s', chapter in Nick Ritchie and Paul Rogers, *The Political Road to War:*

Bush, 9/11 and the Drive to Overthrow Saddam Hussein (Routledge: London and New York, 2006).

13 Edward Walker, *Testimony Before Senate Committee on Foreign Relations*, 22 March 2000, US Senate Committee on Foreign Relations, Washington DC.

14 John Bolton, 'Our Pitiful Iraq Policy', *The Weekly Standard*, 21 December 1998.

CHAPTER 2   THE US MILITARY POSTURE

1 Statement by James Woolsey at Senate Hearings on his appointment as Director of Central Intelligence, Washington DC, February 1993.

2 At its peak, the US nuclear stockpile exceeded 32,000 in the mid-1960s and the Soviet stockpile reached nearly 40,000 in the mid-1980s. See Robert S. Norris and William M. Arkin, 'Global Nuclear Stockpiles, 1945–1997', *The Bulletin of the Atomic Scientists*, November–December 1997.

3 For a general account of the Maritime Strategy, see Norman Friedman, *The US Maritime Strategy* (Jane's Publishers: London, 1988).

4 James D. Watkins, 'The Maritime Strategy', supplement to the *Proceedings of the US Naval Institute*, January 1986.

5 Ibid.

6 This incident came to light some years afterwards. See John D. Gresham, 'Navy Area Ballistic Missile Defense Coming On Fast', *Proceedings of the US Naval Institute*, January 1999.

7 Paul Rogers, 'Towards an Ideal Weapon? Military and Political Implications of the Airborne and Space-based Lasers', *Defense Analysis*, 17(1), 2001: 73–88.

8 An impressively detailed account of the development of the Iraqi chemical and biological weapons prior to the 1991 war, including details of the actual deployment of offensive systems during the war, is to be found in a 1995 report of the UN Special Commission on Iraq (UNSCOM) to the UN Security Council: 'Report of the Secretary-General on the Status of the Implementation of the Special Commission's Plans for Ongoing Monitoring and Verification of Iraq's Compliance with Relevant Parts of Section C of Security Council Resolution 687 (1991)',

New York: UN Security Council report S/1995/684, 11 October
1995. For a detailed overview of the work of UNSCOM, see
Graham S. Pearson, *The Search for Iraq's Weapons of Mass
Destruction: Inspection, Verification and Non-Proliferation*
(Palgrave Macmillan: Basingstoke and New York, 2005).

9 The fact that US intelligence agencies were aware of the Iraqi
regime's willingness to use such WMD systems came to light in
1996 when the US Department of Defense made available on the
internet a large number of reports and studies relating to the
1991 war. These included, by mistake, a classified report relating
to a National Intelligence Estimate of November 1990, two
months before the start of the war. This was subsequently
removed from the website but not before it had been seen by a
number of analysts.

10 Bill Gertz, 'Miracle in the Desert', *Air Force Magazine*, January
1997.

11 William H. McMichael, 'Desert Stronghold', *Air Force Magazine*,
February 1999.

CHAPTER 3   OIL AND THE WAR ON TERROR

1 For an account of the early development of the oil industry,
see Daniel Yergin, *The Prize* (Simon and Schuster: New York,
1993).

2 Two works that discuss issues of oil and security of supply are
Michael Klare, *Blood and Oil* (Hamish Hamilton: London and
New York, 2004), and Toby Shelley, *Oil, Politics, Poverty and the
Planet* (Zed Books: London, 2005). One of the very few analyses
of the role of oil in US policy towards Iraq is Atif Kubursi, 'Oil
and the Global Economy', chapter in Rick Fawn and Raymond
Hinnebusch (eds), *The Iraq War: Causes and Consequences*
(Lynne Rienner: Boulder and London, 2006). Political aspects
of the world oil industry are discussed in Bulent Gokay (ed.),
The Politics of Oil: A Survey (Routledge: London and New York,
2006).

3 *Oil Fields as Military Objectives: A Feasibility Study*, Report to the
Special Subcommittee on Investigations of the House Committee
on International Relations, Congressional Research Service,
Washington DC, August 1975.

4 The Organization of the Joint Chiefs of Staff, *US Military Posture for FY 1982*, US Government Printing Office, Washington DC, 1981.
5 Ibid.

CHAPTER 4   FROM KABUL TO BAGHDAD

1 Osama bin Laden, 'To Our Brothers in Pakistan', in Bruce Lawrence (ed.), *Messages to the World: The Statements of Osama bin Laden* (Verso: London and New York, 2005).
2 Osama bin Laden, 'The Winds of Change', in Bruce Lawrence, op. cit.
3 Ibid.
4 Shaun Gregory, 'The ISI and the War on Terrorism', *Studies in Conflict and Terrorism*, 30(12), December 2007.
5 For a week-by-week contemporary analysis of the war in Afghanistan, see Paul Rogers, *A War on Terror: Afghanistan and After* (Pluto Press: London and Ann Arbor, 2003).
6 See 'America's Theatre in the World', 24 December 2001, in Paul Rogers, *A War on Terror*.
7 Ibid.
8 President George W. Bush, State of the Union address, January 2002, www.whitehouse.gov/stateoftheunion/2002/; accessed 18 May 2007.
9 Ibid.
10 Ibid.
11 Ibid.
12 Ibid.
13 President George W. Bush, Graduation Speech at US Military Academy, West Point, 1 June 2002, www.whitehouse.gov/news/releases/2002/06/20020601-3.html; accessed 18 May 2007.
14 Ibid.
15 Ibid.
16 Walden Bello, 'Endless War?', Focus on the Global South, Manila, September 2001, available at www.focusweb.org/publications/2001/endless_war.html; accessed 10 October 2001.
17 'Autumn 2001: A Watershed in North–South Relations?', *South Letter*, vols 3 and 4, 2001 (The South Centre, Geneva).

CHAPTER 5   BAGHDAD AND BEYOND

1 Thom Shanker and Eric Schmitt, 'Pentagon Expects Long-Term Access to Four Key Bases in Iraq', *New York Times*, 19 April 2003. One of the four possible bases would be at the Baghdad International Airport, a second would be at Tallil near Nasiriya in the south, close to the southern oilfields, a third would be at Bashur in the north, within reach of the oilfields on the Kirkuk–Mosul axis, and a fourth would be at the H-1 base, towards the Syrian border and in a strategically significant position should oil reserves be discovered in the western desert. Some reports shortly after the start of the war suggested that final troop deployments might number as few as 5,000, on the assumption that Iraq would be primarily under the control of the Iraqi government, even if US influence would persist. As the insurgency developed, the Baghdad Airport base became less secure and many of the military facilities were deployed to Balad airbase and the surrounding area, in more open country to the north of Baghdad.

2 The Iraq Body Count group has provided a monitoring of civilian casualties, using a methodology that requires two independent media reports of individual casualties (www.iraqbodycount.org; accessed 6 June 2007). It inevitably does not include unreported deaths but provides a robust baseline. Other figures based on surveys suggest much higher casualty rates of well in excess of 100,000 deaths.

3 General Barry R. MacCaffrey, 'No Choice: Stay the Course in Iraq', *Los Angeles Times*, 3 April 2007.

4 According to the London-based International Institute for Strategic Studies assessing the war in late 2004, 'the government faces an insurgency estimated between 20,000 and 50,000 strong. These fighters are organised in as many as 70 cells, operating largely independently and at best with attenuated coordination. With no coherent centre of gravity and no overall leadership, the insurgency cannot be defeated merely by the application of brute force.' MacCaffrey (note 3) suggests a total of 100,000 insurgents. These figures are not necessarily at variance, given the development of the insurgency between late 2004 and early 2007.

5 Paul Rogers, 'US Plans for Military Expansion', *Open Democracy*, 1 July 2004.

6 Barbara Opall-Rome, 'US–Israel Army Brass Swap Tactics, Secret Meeting Focuses on Anti-Terror War, FCS Technology', *Defense News*, Washington DC, 15 December 2003.

7 Ibid.

8 Barbara Opall-Rome, 'Israeli Arms, Gear Aid US Troops', *Defense News*, Washington DC, 30 March 2004.

9 Ibid.

10 David Brooks, 'A War of Narratives', *International Herald Tribune*, 10 April 2007.

11 Pamela Constable, 'A Wrong Turn, Chaos and a Rescue', *Washington Post*, 15 April 2004.

12 Ibid.

13 Ronald Glasser, 'A Shock Wave of Brain Injuries', *Washington Post*, 8 April 2007.

14 A perceptive analysis of the situation in early 2007 is Toby Dodge, 'The Causes of US Failure in Iraq', *Survival*, 49(1), Spring 2007: 85–106.

15 For a week-by-week analysis of the Iraq War from March 2003 to August 2005, see Paul Rogers, *A War too Far: Iraq, Iran and the New American Century* (Pluto Press: London and Ann Arbor, 2006).

CHAPTER 6 TOWARDS THE LONG WAR

1 For a succinct account of bin Laden's history and the early origins of al-Qaida, see Bruce Lawrence's introduction to the speeches and statements of bin Laden: Bruce Lawrence (ed.), *Messages to the World: The Statements of Osama bin Laden* (Verso: London and New York, 2005). The best overall account of al-Qaida remains Jason Burke, *Al-Qaeda: the True Story of Radical Islam* (Penguin Books: London, 2007). See also Peter Bergen, *The Holy War Inc.: Inside the Secret World of Osama bin Laden* (The Free Press: Phoenix, 2002). A more historical sweep is provided by Charles Allen, *God's Terrorists: The Wahhabi Cult and the Hidden Roots of Modern Jihad* (Abacus: London, 2006).

2 Bruce Lawrence, op. cit.

3 See Gregory (chapter 4, note 4).

4 According to a Washington media report, an analysis from the National Counterterrorism Center entitled *Al-Qaida Better*

Positioned to Strike the West, the network 'is gaining strength and has established a safe haven in remote tribal areas of western Pakistan for training and planning attacks', Spencer S. Hsu and Walter Pincus, 'U.S. Warns of Stronger Al-Qaeda', *Washington Post*, 12 July 2007.

5 See MacCaffrey (chapter 5, note 3).

CHAPTER 7 SUSTAINABLE SECURITY

1 John T. Bennett, 'DoD: Force Planning Built For Irregular, Lengthy Conflicts', *Defense News*, 16 April 2007.

2 Quoted in Bennett, op. cit.

3 The military and political significance of directed energy weapons has substantial relevance to the future US military posture. Even in the late 1990s, this was recognized in a US Air Force study, Directed Energy Applications for Tactical Air Combat (DEATAC). According to the Chair of that study, former USAF Chief of Staff General Ronald R. Fogelman: 'I believe that directed-energy weapons will be fundamental to the way the Air Force fights future wars. This study, which I am pleased to be part of, will help prepare us for the changing face of warfare. It is an important step in pursuing the potential of directed-energy technologies.' See 'Directed Energy Study Kicks Off', *Air Force Research Laboratory Office of Public Affairs DE Release No. 98–32*, Kirtland Air Force Base, New Mexico, 26 June 1998. For a detailed discussion see Paul Rogers, 'Towards an Ideal Weapon? Military and Political Implications of the Airborne and Space-based Lasers', *Defense Analysis*, 17(1), 2001: 73–88.

4 Bill Sweetman, 'Any Time, Any Place, Anywhere: US Puts Emphasis on Prompt Global Strike Ability', *Jane's International Defence Review*, April 2007: 60–5.

5 *Quadrennial Defense Review*, Department of Defense, Washington DC, January 2006, available at www.defenselink.mil/qdr/; accessed 28 May 2007.

6 For example, in March 2007, the US Army War College funded a two-day conference on 'The National Security Implications of Climate Change' at the Triangle Institute in North Carolina. See Juliet Eiperin, 'Military Sharpens Focus on Climate Change', *Washington Post*, 15 April 2007.

7 *Global Strategic Trends 2007–2036*, Development, Concepts and Doctrine Centre, Shrivenham, 2007.

8 This section seeks to summarize a more detailed analysis developed by the Oxford Research Group: Chris Abbott, Paul Rogers and John Sloboda, 'Global Responses to Global Threats: Sustainable Security for the 21st Century', *ORG Briefing Paper*, June 2006, Oxford Research Group, London. This was subsequently developed into a short book, *Beyond Terror*, by the same authors, published by the Rider Books division of Random House, April 2007.

9 These issues are explored in greater depth in chapter 4, 'The New Security Paradigm', in Paul Rogers, *Losing Control: Global Security in the 21st Century* (Pluto Press: London and Ann Arbor, 2002).

10 James Davies, Susanna Sandstrom, Anthony Shorrocks and Edward N. Wolff, 'The World Distribution of Household Wealth', *WIDER Angle*, no. 2, 2006, World Institute for Development Economics Research, Helsinki.

11 One of the early accounts of this issue was David Rind, 'Drying Out the Tropics', *New Scientist*, 6 May 1995.

12 Although the reports of the Intergovernmental Panel on Climate Change have sounded frequent warnings, they tend to be consensus documents, primarily to ensure a degree of scientific authority. One effect is to err on the side of caution whereas there are indications that climate change is actually happening faster than predicted by the IPCC. An example is the rate of melting of Arctic sea ice where there are indications that this is, on average, happening at three times the rate predicted by the eighteen climate models used by the IPCC. See Richard A. Lovett, 'Arctic Ice Melting Much Faster Than Predicted', *National Geographic News*, 1 May 2007.

13 Edwin Brooks, 'The Implications of Ecological Limits to Growth in Terms of Expectations and Aspirations in Developed and Less Developed Countries', chapter in Anthony Vann and Paul Rogers (eds), *Human Ecology and World Development* (Plenum Press: London and New York, 1974).

14 For a discussion on the approaches to security studies, see Alan Collins (ed.), *Contemporary Security Studies* (Oxford University Press: Oxford and New York, 2007).

Index